Copyright © 2026 by Dwight Kopp & Doe Kopp

All rights reserved.

No portion of this book may be reproduced, stored in a retrieval system, or transmitted in any form or by any means—electronic, mechanical, photocopying, recording, or otherwise—without prior written permission from the publisher, except as permitted by U.S. copyright law.

Scripture quotations taken from the Amplified Bible (AMP), Copyright © 2015 by The Lockman Foundation. Used by permission. All rights reserved.

ISBN: 979-8-9946642-0-9

Library of Congress Control Number: 2026902556

Published by

Dwight Kopp

Maytown, PA

For more resources, visit primalchurch.org

First edition

Primal Church

Dwight & Doe Kopp

Contents

Dedication	1
1. Section I	2
2. To See, or Not to See	3
3. Then vs. Now	7
4. What Happened	18
5. Paradigm Shift	28
6. Section II	38
7. Christian Caste System	39
8. Ragamuffin Priests	43
9. Carry the Fire	49
10. Furniture Matters	53
11. Scriptural Model	57
12. Prophet's Reward	63
13. Leadership	67
14. Section III	73
15. The Mission	74
16. Tikkun Olam	80

17.	Rapture?	84
18.	Section IV	88
19.	Intimacy and Influence	89
20.	Shifting Realities	93
21.	Section V	96
22.	Now What?	97
23.	Sacred Cows	102
24.	Defining Church	107
25.	Recommended Reading	110
Acknowledgements		112
About the author		113

To the hidden people—
You may have left the building but not the faith.
You dare to question the status quo and are often found wounded beneath a pile of rocks.
Though discarded, disqualified, and invalidated, you pursue the mystery of the manifest presence of Christ.
You are essential to what God is doing.

SECTION 1
To See Clearly

To See, or Not to See

Several years ago, our youngest (six-year-old) son woke up sick and called for help. My wife, Doe, rushed to him in the bathroom. But on her way back to bed, she passed out and collapsed on the floor. By the time I got to her, Doe had lost bladder control and stopped breathing.

Everything that was important suddenly became irrelevant. Everything else disappeared and the urgency of one single need crowded my vision like a hot white light.

In that moment, only one thing mattered.

Only one thing was essential.

She. Must. Breathe!

I scrambled to the floor, calling her name, desperate for signs of life. Then, cradling her head in my hands, I leaned in and breathed my own life into her. Her chest rose but then all the air came out in a rush, and she lay still.

The night before, all six of us had gone to bed with headaches. I got up in the wee hours, unable to sleep. Following a hunch, I did some research on carbon monoxide poisoning. Everything suggested that our house was too old and drafty for that to be the issue.

Pacified, I went back to sleep.

Now at 5 am, I was kneeling on the floor—my wife dying right in front of me.

When someone stops breathing, seconds matter.

I called for our daughters to grab the phones. Whitney, to call 911 on the cell. Emily, to get the house phone and call our friends. I knew we were either going to the hospital, or the morgue.

Then, I leaned in again—face to face, lips to lips, and breathed into my wife, willing her to live.

Her chest rose and fell. And then rose again!

Whitney handed me the cell. I wasn't thinking clearly; I gave dispatch the wrong house number.

By the time I made it downstairs, I found Emily collapsed on the kitchen floor. Suddenly, through the fog in my brain, a lightbulb came on. I dragged Emily onto the front porch to get fresh air and hollered for our two boys.

Then dispatch—still on the line—requested our correct address. Within minutes, three ambulances and two firetrucks descended on our home.

All six of us were taken to the hospital.

That's the problem with carbon monoxide. You can't see it. You can't taste it. And you can't smell it.

But you can see the effects.

Most people who die from carbon monoxide poisoning notice the symptoms, chalk it up to the flu, and go back to bed.

They never wake up.

In a later conversation with our first responder, he told me his carbon monoxide meter maxed out as soon as he stepped through the door.

"At those levels," he said, "you have three minutes to live."

The fact that we were alive at all was the grace of God.

Just as my wife lay without breath, so modern church might look good, sound good, and do good things, but the breath of God is largely absent. We no longer see the power of the Holy Spirit that was normal in the early church.

Perhaps you, too, are waking up to the reality that something has gone terribly wrong. You've wondered why we don't experience an Acts 2 fellowship.

Maybe you, too, want to experience everything Christ had in mind for us, His Bride.

I want to live out a faith like that described in the New Testament. I want to know and walk in the power of the resurrected Christ! What I'm chasing is the Primal Church: Fellowship with Christ and believers walking in the power and authority as God intended.

To find that, we need to go back to our roots to wrinkle out what Christ had in mind.

It's time to put everything on the table.

To see—to really apprehend— what is holding us back is the first step. Seeing what is broken is the beginning of breakthrough. Truth sets us free.

We can't fix anything if we won't take a hard look at the status quo. We can't honor Christ if we cover up the broken and pretend that everything is fine. Honor does not avoid real issues in an effort to 'keep the peace' or maintain appearances. Honor confronts with love and invites others into God's best. Honor and transparency welcome the Spirit of Truth. God gave us the gift of discernment for a reason! If we're unwilling to see what strongholds currently keep the Bride captive, we will be left with a sleeping beauty.

In the following section, we will compare the early church with the modern church, then we'll take a look at what happened, what we're missing, and why it matters.

Then vs. Now

According to historians, the early church existed between Pentecost and the year 312 AD. That said, we will define the early church more by *how* it functioned than by *when* it was around. While the early church had her share of issues, their expression of Christianity was more consistent with what God had in mind.

In order to compare the modern church with how the primal church expressed the nature of Christ, we need to ask a few simple questions. The answers might seem obvious, but sometimes what is most important can be hidden right in front of us.

Read slowly. Chew on each item. Take it in. Let it nourish the quest that brought you to this little book. Dig through the unnecessary trappings of your faith and ask God to help you find the treasure hidden beneath all of it. You can jot down your own responses or entertain yourself with mine.

As we consider the following, think in terms of furniture, function and faith.

What did the early church have?

They had a general capacity to operate in the miraculous—including healing the sick, casting out demons and raising the dead.

According to Hyatt, notables of the early church era, including Justin Martyr (AD 100-165), Irenaeus (AD 125-200), Tertullian (AD 160-240), Origen (AD 185-284), Cyprian (AD 195-258) and Novatian (AD 210-280), all testified that miraculous expressions of the Holy Spirit were part of 'normal' Christianity during the first three hundred years.[1]

The early church had limited access to the Scripture.

Most estimates put literacy rates at less than 10% with many suggesting only 3%. Access to any kind of printed media was extremely limited. Oral tradition (memorization) was strong.

While the early church had spiritual leaders, all believers ministered to one another.

Paul encouraged everyone in the early church to function as an essential part of the ministering body when they came together.

The early church experience was primarily a home-based fellowship with meals, music, testimonies, words of prophesy, healing, mutual encouragement and prayer.

Fellowship with other believers happened anywhere. But generally speaking, people gathered often in each-other's homes. See Acts 2:46, 5:42, 12:12, Romans 16:3-5, 1 Corinthians 16:19, Colossians 4:15, Philemon 1:2.

---

1. Hyatt, E.L. (2015). 2000 Years of Charismatic Christianity Charisma Media.

The early church understood the cost of following Christ.

We don't have to read too far into the book of Acts to notice the growing persecution. The long history of Rome's oppression of Christians underscored the high price people paid for their faithfulness.

The early church functioned with a profound dependence on the Holy Spirit.

The prevalence of the miraculous indicates an intimacy and reliance on the Holy Spirit. This included looking to Him for leadership decisions, filling with courage, power, prophetic direction, healing, deliverance and solutions to daily life. (Here are only some of those references: Acts 2:1-4, 4:31, 8:29, 10:19-20, 11:12, 13:2-4, 13:2-4, 16:6-7)

The early church meetings were a believers-only fellowship.

While early believers certainly shared the good news, their times of fellowship were reserved for believers. Fellowship was not an outreach. It was a time of intimate connection with Christ in each other. (Acts 5:13)

Continual hospitality was the norm for the early church.

The Jewish celebratory feasts set the cultural backdrop for the early corporate experience. Hospitality was baked into Old Testament law (Leviticus 19:33-34 and Deuteronomy 10:18-19) and the New Testament gives many exhortations to practice hospitality.

There were multiple directives to eat together.

The early church often made spiritual decisions as a group.

Generally speaking, there was a lot more all-together-ness in the early church. People needed each other more in that time and culture.

Why? Because Eastern culture lived connected to their community.

Early believers considered themselves individual parts of the same body—not lone sailors. They recognized that one person's choice could impact everyone.

Five multi-generational households are specifically mentioned as experiencing salvation at the same time. (John 4:53, Acts 10:44-48, Acts 16:14-15, Acts 16:31-34, 1 Corinthians 1:16)

The early church walked in reverence for the LORD.

The early church held a deep sense of awe toward God and His ways. Respect for the LORD fueled discipleship growth. (Acts 9:31) This reverence seems to be a pre-set for encountering the work of Christ in the fellowship of believers. (Acts 5:4,11, Hebrews 12:28-29, Philippians 2:12-13)

Leaders in the early church were chosen because they were spiritually mature.

Leaders were full of the Holy Spirit. Their godly character was known by the way they managed their families or their businesses. Leaders were recognized by their speech, life, love, faith, hope and purity. (1 Timothy 4:12). They were not, however, chosen because they did miracles!

Resumes, diplomas and degrees were never leadership considerations. In fact, Paul made much of the worthlessness of his own religious attainments and education compared to the value of Christ's work in him. (Philippians 3:4-11)

The early church recognized more than twelve apostles.

A quick internet search for *apóstolos* in the New Testament will give you a list of about twenty.

The early church weren't opposed to female leaders.

This list includes, but is not limited to, the teacher Priscilla, Junia the apostle (Rom 16:7), and Photini (the woman at the well), an evangelist.

They had a keen understanding that the advance of God's kingdom and personal purity were connected.

When the Israelites gave themselves to idolatry, they were oppressed or taken into captivity. As a result, the early church understood that their capacity to extend the King's influence was connected to personal and corporate purity. (1 Corinthians 6:9-10, Galatians 5:19-21, Ephesians 5:5-6)

Paul noted that individual sin impacted the whole body. (See 1 Corinthians 11:27-30) Early Christians were instructed to handle discipline, sickness and burden-bearing as a group. Paul told the Corinthians not to eat with someone who claimed to belong to Christ yet lived in flagrant disobedience. (1 Cor. 5:11) Jesus even called out groups of believers in Revelation 2-3 for passive tolerance of sin.

You could say, everyone was held responsible for everyone.

The early church understood that the mission of Christ was to restore all creation—not just to rescue mankind from hell.

The early church did not confuse Kingdom (the mission) with Paradise (part of the benefit package). They understood that Christ came to restore *everything* corrupted by the fall of man.

What has been added that the early church did not have?

We added 'Church' buildings.

If I say, I'll meet you in the church parking lot, you know exactly what I mean. Why? Today 'church' refers to a building. Christians (collectively) can claim more real estate than any other organization on the planet (certain royal dynasties excepted). Along with this comes mortgages, building committees, and facility managers.

I hear people say that they know church isn't a building. But language reveals culture, and our language betrays us.

Remember, when the New Testament speaks of the church, it never refers to a building or denomination.

Not once. Ever.

We have since added programs.

In the early church, no one came together for fellowship with an order of service. Believers most often gathered around a table. They ate together regularly. No one divided the time into worship, sermon, ministry time. No bulletins, no spotlights, no microphones, no pulpits and no platforms. No one was tied to the clock!

In the early church, the order of service was decided by the Holy Spirit. (1 Cor. 12:4-11)

We made pastors the central feature in our church experience.

Now 'pastor' has become an identity, a title, a position, and a career path.

The early church wasn't built around a pastor or any single leader. The pastoral gift was *just one of the many* ways the Holy Spirit was represented in the fellowship. In fact, the word 'pastor' only appears once or twice in the entire New Testament. Leaders did not hold positions. Each person simply walked in the gifts God gave them.

We added children's church and Sunday School.

In the early church, children were part of the fabric of adult life. They were pretty much part of everything. The early church didn't separate out the children so the parents could listen to a pastor speak.

We added youth groups.

Stanley Hall invented the idea of adolescence around 1904, but Jewish youths were considered adults at the age of twelve or thirteen. As such, they were actually expected to participate as contributing members of society.

We added pews.

More specifically, we added the practice of spectating instead of participating. The new rules were 1) face front and 2) be quiet.

We added ushers.

What? How did the early Christians earn their merit badges?

The spiritual gift of 'ushing' is never mentioned in the Holy Writ.

We added sermons.

Teaching happened spontaneously as people asked questions about real-life situations where discipleship was needed. Many of Paul's epistles are answers to questions he was asked in previous letters (not in Scripture).

Occasionally believers heard from a traveling apostles or teacher who came to town—but sermons and teaching were never the centerpiece of their fellowship.

Teaching in the Primal Church was primarily an unrehearsed, Spirit-led and informal expression. Whenever believers met together, anyone there might share what God was teaching them. Everyone leaned in and honored the gift others brought. (Col. 3:16, Rom. 12:4-5, 1 Thess. 5:11)

Can you tell me the high points from the last three sermons you heard? Today, the sermon alone accounts for almost 50 hours per year of your annual "church" experience.

We added pulpits.

Most early believers met in homes. Most homes don't have pulpits. A pulpit in a living room is, after all, a wee bit awkward. I'm pretty sure my wife doesn't want one. I've never heard of a family gathering that included one!

Just sayin'.

Pulpits came when Christians were divided into clergy and laity. The clergy were elevated so we could hear them; the laity were expected to observe in silence.

We added coffee.

Now considered essential to life, this heavenly brew was not available to the early church. In fact it took another 1400 years to manifest.

But they had wine. So, not terrible.

We added greeters.

See previous merit badge concern.

We added salaried and paid staff.

The early church had no paid CEO, no worship leaders, no youth pastors, nor pastors of visitation or outreach. Occasionally an apostle, prophet, evangelist, or teacher received a financial contribution, but no one collected a salary. (1 Tim. 5:17-18, 1 Cor. 9:14) Jesus told his disciples to give without cost what they had received for free. (Matt. 10:8)

Even Paul, credited with writing almost one-quarter of the New Testament, sometimes worked as a tentmaker so as not to be a burden to the people he served. While he occasionally received financial assistance, Paul's service to his fellow believers cost *him* dearly—not the other way around.

Regular, salaried positions in the church began much later with state-funded clergy.

We created ministerial degrees and divinity programs.

Today, leaders are primarily vetted by their resume and credentialed by an institution. In the early church, professional Christians didn't exist, neither did the institutions that qualify 'professional' Christians.

Jesus picked fisherman, tax collectors, restored prostitutes and zealots as his students and friends. No titles. No hooded robes. No cap. No gown with degree-specific regalia. People knew you spent time with Jesus because you acted like Him.

From Pentecost onward, leaders were empowered by the Holy Spirit and recognized because of their service, character, and faith.

We now have easy access to Scripture.

Portions of the Old Testament were accessible to those close to the temple in Jerusalem or a synagogue, but (almost) no one had their own copy. In fact, according to historians, many synagogues didn't even have a complete copy of the Old Testament.

During the first century, believers occasionally got a letter from an apostle in reply to specific questions or concerns. These would be read at their gatherings and then shared with area fellowships. (Remember the earlier mention of literacy rates.)

Gutenberg hadn't been born yet. He didn't figure out the movable type printing press until 1440. Books (as we know them) were non-existent. Written material was expensive to produce.

And yet Christ came at *just the right time* in history.

We added hymnals and LED screens.

Believers in the early years sang Psalms or hymns they had memorized or sang "spiritual songs" which they made up themselves.

We added sound systems.

Hard to imagine that the majority of Christian history has been absent this cool piece of hardware. So how did the early mega churches function without it?

Ah. You're right. They didn't have mega churches either.

We added bookstores and merchandise.

See previous discussion about Gutenberg. The early church had no WWJD wrist bands. No bumper stickers. No *Jesus Saves* hoodies.

No gold-cross necklaces. How in the world did other people know they were followers of Jesus?

We added the stage.

Meetings were small enough that everyone could see and hear everyone else.

We added online church.

Too obvious?

The early church believed that you actually can't encourage one another if you are by yourself. (Heb. 10:25)

We now welcome unbelievers into church.

In the beginning, the unsaved and carnal believers were not part of Christian fellowship. (1 Cor. 2:10-16; 2 Cor. 6:14-18)

Because of frequent persecution, people only joined a fellowship if they were serious about following Christ.

This doesn't mean the unbelievers weren't loved, just that they didn't participate in the fellowship of believers.

We added outreach programs.

The modern industry of religion is very concerned about fire insurance. Yes, the early church went after the lost, but their mission wasn't just "saving souls."

We added a new read on the rapture.

The idea of Christians being swept away to Paradise only started in the 1800's. Look up the work of John Nelson Darby to learn more.

The early church believed there would come a day when the *unrighteous* are swept away and the lovers of God would inherit the earth. (Matt. 24:37-41; Matt. 13:30, 40-43, 49-50; Ps. 37:9-11, 20, 22, 28-29, 36, 38)

While we've only just scratched the surface, it's pretty clear that precious little of what we call normal church today is anything like the early church. In fact, if you were to strip away everything that's been added, many of our modern churches would be left with nothing at all.

Our goal over the next few chapters is to briefly unpack how we ended up here, what we lost along the way, and (most of all) *why it matters*.

What Happened

How did we end up here? It's plain to see our modern experience of "church" holds little similarity to the early-church.

A brief summary of early church history can help us understand how we ended up here. This is not meant to be a comprehensive or authoritative historical account. Instead, this is simply a survey of key events and trends—as best we can reconstruct them since there are notable variations in historical accounts.

So what happened?

303 to 311 — During this period, Roman emperor Diocletian unleashed another round of severe Christian persecution. The persecution was merciless and barbaric. Almost every follower of Christ knew someone who had been killed, maimed or dismembered for their faith. I'll spare you the details. But there are also stories of amazing miracles and staggering faith. Stories of lions and bears that wouldn't kill Christians. [1]

311 — The Edict of Serdica (also known as the Edict of Toleration by Galerius) ended the persecution which started under Diocletian—the most intense persecution under Roman rule. Some accounts suggest the Roman regional leadership had their fill of violence. When we consider that violence was Rome's favorite entertainment, we get a glimpse of the level of terror to which believers were subjected.

Still, Christians were considered a pariah and remained impoverished.[2]

312 — Constantine went to battle against a rival emperor, Maxentius. Legend has it Constantine sought divine aid. He saw a cross superimposed over the sun and heard the words, 'conquer by this.'[3] From that point on, Constantine appears to have believed Christ was an incarnation of Mithras, the sun god.

---

1. *The Tenth Persecution, Under Dicoletian, A.D. 303 – Fox's Book of Martyrs.* (n.d.). Biblestudytools.com.https://www.biblestudytools.com/history/foxs-book-of-martyrs/the-tenth-persecution-under-diocletian-a-d-3-3.html

2. *Edictum Galerii (English Translation).* (n.d.). Droitromain.univ-Grenoble-Alpes.fr.https://droitromain.univ-grenoble-alpes.fr/Anglica/ed_tolerat1_engl.htm

3. Hudson, M., & Britannica Editors. (2025, October 21). Battle of the Milvian Bridge. Encyclopedia Britannica. https://www.britannica.com/topic/Battle-of-the-Milvian-Bridge

Mithras also happened to be the god of war, so it made a convenient mix. Depending on what version of history you read, Mithras was said to have been born of a virgin, Anahita, the fertility goddess. Some have suggested Anahita means 'undefiled' or 'immaculate.'

Sound familiar?

Nevertheless, Constantine called himself a Christ follower. Quite suddenly, prospects for believers under Roman rule completely changed.

Christians breathed a collective sigh.

313 — Shortly after defeating Maxentius, Constantine issued the Edict of Milan, ushering in the "Peace of the Church"—an official decree of toleration for Christians. This edict granted the return of confiscated property, more restoration of religious freedom, and special privileges to followers of Christ.[4] While Romans continued to despise Jews, the longstanding cultural hatred and animosity toward Christians ended. Within two years, Christians went from being hunted like animals to being granted favored political status.

The relief must have been staggering.

Suddenly they no longer had to fear for their lives or the lives of their families. No longer did they face the prospect of horrible death, sadistic torture and public humiliation.

In a striking about face, Christianity became a means of financial and social advancement. With gifts and favors, Constantine enticed

---

4. Hyatt, E.L. (2002). *2000 Years of Charismatic Christianity* (p.33). Charisma House.

the wealthy Roman elite to convert.[5] Being a Christian became politically expedient.

As a result, a massive influx of godless idolators polluted the fellowship of believers.

321 — Nine years after his conversion, Constantine demonstrated the quality of his devotion to Christ by naming the first day of the week, Sunday, after Mithras, the sun god. Furthermore, he continued minting official coinage with the image of himself and the sun-god until 324.[6]

324 — Twelve years after purportedly choosing the way of Christ, Constantine murdered his son Crispus and Fausta (his second wife). Apparently, the two had an affair and Fausta may have been pregnant as a result. Either way, by Constantine's order she was killed in a hot bath and Crispus was poisoned.[7]

325 — Constantine called the First Council of Nicaea in order to centralize his control of Christianity.[8]

---

5. Pierce, C., & Heidler, R. (2015). *The Apostolic Church Arising* (pp. 43-44) Glory of Zion International Ministries, Inc.

6. Viola, F., Barna, G. (2012). *Pagan Christianity?* (p. 19). Tyndale. (Original work published 2002)

7. Woods, D. (1998). On the Death of Empress Fausta. *Greece and Rome, 45*(1), 70-86. https://doi.org/10.1093/gr/45.1.70

8. Pierce, C., & Heidler, R. (2015). *The Apostolic Church Arising* (p. 44). Glory of Zion International Ministries, Inc.

This was the year he named himself Pontifex Maximus, high priest of the church and Rome.[9] The New Testament is pretty clear that there is only one High Priest, but the church said nothing.

This moment was a hinge point in history, when the Church and State merged into one political entity.

Constantine also circulated his opinion that Christians distance themselves from Jews and their holy days by refusing to celebrate the Sabbath and the Resurrection of Christ on Passover. He wrote, "Let us have nothing in common with the detestable Jewish crowd."[10] Considering the church's backstory with Rome, an imperial recommendation would have been considered by many as tantamount to law.

Until then many believers observed the Sabbath. Now, instead of the home-centered, interactive fellowship, they were "encouraged" to attend ritualistic services in basilicas that included shrines, altars, images, priests, processions, parades and incense.[11] Instead of spiritual mothers and fathers, believers gathered under emperor-selected leaders to follow a prescribed pattern of worship.

In an effort to establish control under his new religious order, Constantine encouraged the construction and repair of purpose-built places of worship. He instructed governors "not to spare

---

9. Heidler, Dr. R.D. (2006). The Messianic Church Arising! (p. 42). Glory of Zion International Ministries, Inc.

10. (2023). Ccjr.us.https://www.ccjr.us/dialogika-resources/prima ry-texts/constantine-i

11. Viola, F., Barna, G. (2012). Pagan Christianity? (p.19-27). Tyndale. (Original work published 2002)

the expenditure of money, but to draw supplies from the imperial treasury itself" to finance these buildings.[12] But he who pays the piper, calls the tune. His imperial influence extended to the pattern of worship throughout the empire.

The incorporation of pervasive statuary and iconography (which would have been anathema to any Messianic Jew) points to the invasion of Roman paganism with only a thin Christian veneer. Until Constantine, the Jewish influence on Christianity had remained very much intact.

Because Messianic Jews and Christians often celebrated together the resurrection of Christ on Passover, Constantine—who hated the Jews—strongly encouraged the church to celebrate on Easter instead.[13] Easter had long been a pagan holiday when people gave decorated eggs as gifts to commemorate Ishtar, a fertility goddess.

Today, most Christians are largely unaware of the inextricable link between Passover and the death and resurrection of Christ. His crucifixion and resurrection during Passover fulfilled the prophecies of a perfect sacrificial lamb. (John 1:29) Consequently, believers in the early church continued to honor this family-based feast.

---

12. CHURCH FATHERS: Life of Constantine, Book II (Eusebius). (2023). Newadvent.org. https://www.newadvent.org/fathers/24022.htm?

13. (2023). Ccjr.us.https://www.ccjr.us/dialogika-resources/primary-texts/constantine-i

In time, the celebration of Passover and Sabbath became a capital offense under Roman rule.[14]

Constantine casts a long shadow.

326 — Around this time Constantine built Old St. Peter's Basilica.

Traditionally, basilicas were built for two reasons. For emperor worship and for the Roman government to hold court. Emperor worship included a full sensory experience with robes, images, incense, and candles all deliberately designed to intimidate and show who had access to the gods. The emperor stood front and center on a raised dais.

Everyone else stood below and watched.

They were required to remain silent as non-participating spectators.[15] Using this pattern, Constantine completely re-styled and ritualized the form and function of Christian gatherings. He divided Christians into political districts. The building, program and leadership all mirrored Roman political organization and pagan practices. None of these had previously been a part of the church.

The focus shifted from relational interaction to spectating a ceremony.

The Roman government appointed people to positions of church leadership and paid them a salary. Those who conformed with Rome were given positions with privilege, power and prestige. Before, all believers functioned as essential ministers during times of fellowship. Now only the state-selected few could participate while the

---

14. Robert D. Heidler, The Messianic Church Arising!: Restoring the Church to Our Covenental Roots (Heidler, 2006), p. 46.

15. Pierce, C., & Heidler, R. (2015). *The Apostolic Church Arising* (p. 44-45). Glory of Zion International Ministries, Inc.

majority watched. Only priests (clergy) were allowed to interpret Scripture and administer 'sacred' rites.[16]

In fact, in the eyes of the church, they became the gate keepers of Paradise itself.

In Summary

In the space of 15 years, the entire face of Christian fellowship changed so dramatically it would have been completely unrecognizable to an early believer.

Constantine effectively converted an organic fellowship of believers into a political organization with a completely different set of priorities. Small wonder the age of the early church ended somewhere between 312 and 325.

That said, Constantine didn't kill the early church. ***The early church died because believers compromised.*** However, the church beyond the influence of Rome continued to thrive and function as the primal church.[17]

Please understand: I'm profoundly grateful I did not have to live through the persecution suffered by the early church. I can only imagine the relief of suddenly having a Roman emperor who promoted Christianity!

But the collateral damage to the fellowship of believers today cannot be understated.

Before Constantine, early church leaders were (generally) credentialed by their speech, life, love, faith, hope and purity. (1 Tim.

---

16. Pierce, C., & Heidler, R. (2015). *The Apostolic Church Arising* (p. 44-45). Glory of Zion International Ministries, Inc.

17. See Chapter 5 in *The Messianic Church Arising!* by Robert Heidler (2016).

3:1-7) After Constantine, positions of church leadership were a means of gaining social status. Anyone could be chosen (according to favor) and credentialed by the state; it had nothing to do with one's relationship with God.

Before Constantine, the fellowship of believers was home, family, and community based. After Constantine, it digressed into a scripted service.

Before Constantine, discipleship naturally resulted from believers gathering together around a family table. After Constantine, following rules and attending a ceremony became the measure of one's devotion.

Before Constantine, Christianity represented a fellowship of the faithful. After Constantine, it corrupted into a ladder for social climbers.

Before Constantine, all believers ministered to one another. After Constantine, the elevation of clergy destroyed the equality and interactive ministry of all believers.

Before Constantine, the church had the power to heal, cast out demons and raise the dead. After Constantine, the church mutated into a wealthy institution that exalted wealth, knowledge, and power.

This wasn't an accidental shift or the atrophy of time. In under 50 years a vibrant, powerful fellowship of believers devolved into a political organization with no authority over darkness.

In a short period of time, believers lost three foundational understandings:

First

The point and purpose of Christian fellowship is to allow for the expression of the Holy Spirit in every believer.

Second
Our mission is to heal the whole earth. (Rom. 8)
Third
Purity enables us to carry the influence and authority of our King.

Paradigm Shift

Soon after Pentecost, the enemy had a whole litany of Roman rulers lined up to bring trouble to those following the way of Christ. For three hundred years, in varying waves of persecution, the emperors devised every kind of method to harass, kill, maim, and destroy Christians.

By the beginning of the third century, the church was desperate for a reprieve, and the stage was set for the enemy to make his move.

It worked just like the movies. When the FBI brings someone in for interrogation, they often employ the good/cop, bad/cop tactic to gain the psychological advantage. The "bad cop" plays the heavy. Intimidating, aggressive, confrontational. His only job is to create psychological pressure.

Then a second interrogator enters the game.

The "good cop" employs a friendly, supportive persona. Can I get you anything? A drink? A snack? A cigarette?

Suddenly, the prisoner feels extraordinary relief at this unexpected kindness. He relaxes. And the interrogator gets what he wants.

Satan plays this game too.

The "good cop" entered when Emperor Constantine announced his "conversion" to Christianity in the year 312.

I can't imagine the relief believers must have felt. The highest ruler of the land was now on their side. No more living in constant fear for their life and the lives of those they loved. No more hiding in caves and tombs. No more being hunted, tortured, maimed and killed. No longer banned from business, education, housing, or jobs. No longer hated by the general public.

Christianity not only became legal—it was encouraged! Where once they had been hunted like animals and their property confiscated, now the emperor favored Christians in politics, erected temples, and paid full-time leaders.

Constantine dissolved the organic fellowship of believers and encouraged them to meet only in local basilicas.[1] He wanted believers to worship God his way, in his buildings. They were grand and beautiful. A whole new cadre of leaders were employed—paid for by the emperor himself. Titles were given. Buildings (now known as churches) were filled. No more hiding in the catacombs.

He ritualized certain elements of Christianity and recast them as sacred rites performed solely by the religious elite.[2] Formal ceremonies were meant to sway the emotional experience. They looked and felt beautiful.

But not only were his modifications unscriptural, they opposed the very essence of Christianity.

---

1. Philip Schaff: NPNF (V2-02): 0307=281 – Christian Classics Ethereal Library. (2025). Ccel.org. https://www.ccel.org/ccel/schaff/npnf202/Page_281.html

2. Viola, F., & Barna, G. (2012). *Pagan Christianity?: Exploring the roots of our church practices* (pp.16-28). Tyndale House Publishers.

Through it all, the Church lost her heart and the Breath of God. They compromised how they met, where they met, when they met, what they celebrated, and with whom they met.

The intimate communion of Christ followers had been translated into a full-blown religious system. This was not an organizational change but a seismic, cultural shift.

The believers' compromises signaled the end of the Primal Church—the thriving, interactive and dynamic Body of Christ. Those once known for turning the world upside down settled for a neatly packaged religious experience, devoid of the essentials identified in Scripture. Both their active support or passive agreement (remaining silent) allowed religious ideologies to permeate culture.

Since then, we've normalized a kind of Christian fellowship that has no Scriptural precedent. It should not, then, surprise us that our modern fellowship doesn't look anything like the early church.

Religion is slippery like that. This a man-centered and ungodly framework has to be dealt with before we can navigate change. It is a demonic construct that has shaped the (now global) Christian Industrial Complex.

Religion becomes a regional stronghold when groups of people agree (actively or passively) with a paradigm that stands opposed to the word of God. When a town, county, state, or country agree with a flawed idea or broken world view, it becomes an archetype or area-level demonic stronghold. As such, it functions as a cultural overlord for that area.

The religious stronghold often drives the program, leadership, messaging, behaviors and interpersonal relationships for the modern church. While the following facets are not evident in every institutional expression of church, the breakdown may be helpful as you take a personal and corporate inventory.

PROGRAM
Religion says...

A religious spirit works to separate believers by brand, style of music, theological preferences, tone, leadership styles, governing bodies, modesty rules, conduct, comfort and access to good coffee.

And if separating believers by stripe weren't enough, divisions occur inside the building as profoundly as without!

We divide parents from youth and children and infants. People gather together but are rarely able to interact on any meaningful level. Remember, there are rules: Face forward. Follow the leaders. Stay in your place. Keep quiet and listen.

Sadly, we can show up in our Sunday best, hide our baggage and remain indefinitely in a state of apathy or outright disobedience—without risk of exposure or consequence. We can meet and greet, perform and participate, volunteer and sit on boards without ever experiencing intimate fellowship with Christ in each other.

After all the Christian activity, there's precious little time left over for real relationships. Instead of real vulnerability with Christ in each other, we check the box of weekly participation and feel good about ourselves.

Religion suggests we must have established institutions to keep us righteous. It says that without the "covering" of authority, or teaching of the word, we will fall into sin or heresy.

Scripture teaches...

Connecting with Christ in each other is, actually, the essential center-point for believers when they gather. Paul never suggested that attending a weekly service would keep us from evil and protect us from false doctrine. Instead, he writes that participating in spiritual communion where each gift is present and 'does its part' is essential to maturity and protects us from false teaching. (Ephesians 4:14)

LEADERSHIP
Religion says...
Religion disqualifies the priesthood of all believers and establishes a social hierarchy of spiritual gifts. (Hebrews 4:16) It elevates and isolates a select few as ministers, both physically—with titles, clothing, platforms, and pulpits—and financially, by paying them to exercise their spiritual gift. Leaders are set apart from the body instead of being fully among them.

Religion also disqualifies the laity under the guise of safety and correct doctrine (control). Sanctify some, ignore others. Honor some, invalidate others. Credentialing the few disqualifies the rest.

Scripture teaches...
Christ's perfect sacrifice and the torn veil of the old temple granted every believer access to the throne of God. Where religion divided clergy and laity, Christ sanctifies, commissions, and honors every believer as a minister (servant) of the King.

MESSAGING
Religion says...
The core of religion is the belief that our heart is bad and God is generally angry at us. The religious spirit communicates that our natural bent is toward evil. Therefore, we must stay disciplined and keep the rules in order to protect ourselves from sin, which is always crouching at the door. We view our hearts and desires as untrustworthy. We never feel good enough.

The way we see God directly impacts our worldview. The resulting culture of religion is full of judgments, criticism, condemnation and guilt. It is unsafe to be real, to confess, to be vulnerable. Sin therefore, must be hidden. To be known is to be rejected.

In the end, there's no safe place for our humanity, our broken.

This message disregards the plain teaching of scripture.

Scripture teaches...

Salvation is not about getting a ticket to Paradise—salvation is a heart transplant. We are new creatures and can be trusted to listen to and follow God. (See John 14:26) Ezekiel writes, "Moreover, I will give you a new heart and put a new spirit within you, and I will remove the heart of stone and give you a heart of flesh. I will put my Spirit within you and cause you to walk in My statutes, and you will keep My ordinances and do them" (36:26-27). (See also John 10:1-5)

BEHAVIORS

Religion says...

Religion says we must perform to earn God's favor. Just try harder! Being a good Christian is based on man's effort.

Why does religion promote this? Because performance is toxic to authentic relationships and authentic relationship is essential to true fellowship.

Religion binds us to the ever-teetering balancing act between pride and shame. In the performance/shame cycle, I'm proud when I do well and shamed when I mess up. As a result, there are a whole litany of protective measures in place to avoid evil: Attend services, have devotions, pray every day, hold a Bible study, serve in the programs. Don't drink, smoke, or chew or go with girls who do.

Legalism becomes necessary when you believe that a redeemed heart is evil. So religion sets up rules (laws), as a means of procuring favor from God and winning the approval of others.

Religion weaponizes Scripture as a tool for sin management. It uses judgment, criticism, shame, self-punishment, condemnation, self-hatred, and the approval of others as "tools" for spiritual growth.

Having to earn God's blessings creates orphans: Orphans are obsessed with the next meal, the next thing, the next moment—always on alert, always working an angle, grasping to take care of themselves. They work and strive and wither under the scourge of trying to be good enough. They live in fear of never finding love and acceptance.

Bottom line: religion's story is all about sin.

Scripture teaches...

Jesus' story is about redemption, belonging and acceptance. We are chosen, adopted and loved by our Father—redeemed and covered by the righteousness of Christ. **We don't obey so we can be loved, we obey *because* we are loved by our Father.**

INTERPERSONAL RELATIONSHIPS

Religion says...

Religion hates authentic relationship. Instead, it favors the busy, dressed-up, plastic, pretense designed to make everyone think (for a few hours a week) that you have it all together. Have you ever sat next to someone on Sunday mornings, week after week for years, only to discover that their marriage was a sham? Have you ever made friends with someone on a Sunday morning and believed their value system was aligned with Christ, only to find out otherwise later? Our current religious model fosters pretense, hiding, and performance instead of promoting humble and undisguised interaction. Since intimate connection and fellowship with Christ are elemental to personal transformation, religion works to destroy it.

Scripture teaches...

Authentic, face-to-face communion is what fueled the explosive power of the Primal Church.

Christ dwells intimately in every believing individual. The purpose of that indwelling is that we might know Him intimately, personally and corporately. His expressed desire was that His Spirit in us would co-mingle with His Spirit in others.

For example hydrogen and oxygen are, by themselves, complete. But when they come together, a chemical reaction occurs. The synthesis results in a compound—the creation of something entirely new and life-giving: water.

What that synergy creates is not only amazing, it's essential.

In the same way, true communion with other believers results in a 'chemical reaction' where we see a manifestation of Christ that is both powerful, personal, and absolutely essential to life.

CULTURE

Religion says...

Religion focuses on performance: attendance, participation, giving, volunteering, and sin. It shifts our focus from communion to knowledge, from intimacy to activity.

Religion leans toward control, fear, manipulation, intimidation, and favoritism.

"Nice-ness" is also a common fingerprint of the religious spirit. Overlooking key passages in the gospels, this doctrine re-imagines Jesus as the ultimate Mr. Nice Guy. Niceianity says we must be "nice" to everyone all the time. We cannot make or hold a boundary. We have to justify "no" as an answer. We cannot say, "This hurt me," because that might hurt someone!

And that isn't nice.

You will recognize this spirit at play, because the injustice that results leads those who are frustrated to take things into their own hands. When someone gets hurt, rather than having a conversation leading to restoration, the hurt person takes it to the prayer chain. You know what I'm talking about: the prayer request that spiritualizes revenge, gossip, slander, and the total decimation of a person's character.

The religious playbook forbids rocking the boat, asking hard questions, and the general ruffling of feathers. Keep the status quo. Avoid conflict. Don't make anyone upset. Don't ever be visibly angry.

And for heavens sake, do not, under any circumstances, call out sin or confront wrongs in elders or leaders!

Religious leaders tend to hide under Scriptures such as, "Do not touch the LORD's anointed", insinuating or stating outright that "rules are for thee, but not for me". As such, religion creates the perfect petri dish for abusive and narcissistic behavior: controlling, manipulating, bullying, and gaslighting.

The siren of religion stands on the corner, wooing Christians with an easy, no-strings-attached substitute. It functions as a cheap replacement for true connection. Religion corrupts or ritualizes the essentials of true fellowship and retards spiritual growth. It allows us the feels of fellowship, while we stay comfortably hidden behind our masks. No vulnerability. No iron sharpens iron. No one calls anyone up to a greater life. No growth or challenge required.

Nowhere is this more vividly represented than in communion. What began as a potluck and celebratory feast has become a private ritual with a plastic-wrapped wafer and a half-teaspoon of grape syrup in a disposable cup.

We can't step into the more God has for us by switching programs or denominations. Only repentance will demolish the high places where we have made compromises with the spirit of religion.

Repentance is the doorway by which we step back into God's design for the church. It is the way we re-turn to the truth about God, and align with what He says about who we are.

What happened?

We have blindly followed the traditions handed down to us.

What must we do?

Let's ask God to give us a willingness to see what He has in mind for the Church and give ourselves permission to ask hard questions about the religious systems in which we participate.

If you feel uncomfortable with this, ask yourself:

Do I believe that asking questions about the modern expression of church means I'm dishonoring God or His established authority?

Am I afraid of what people will think of me if I ask questions about church or think outside the box?

Am I willing to let go of an unholy loyalty to buildings, brands, traditions and professional Christians?

Why am I afraid of asking questions?

Want more? Visit primalchurch.org for the free download on **Religious Ideologies**.

Section 11
The Priesthood Of All Believers

Christian Caste System

From the beginning, Jesus challenged the religious norms of his day. He didn't pick disciples from the Pharisees or Sadducees (the religious elite). He didn't vet his followers based on their adherence to Mosaic law. He wasn't looking for the best scholars.

He picked fishermen. He chose tax collectors, zealots, and former prostitutes.

And Jesus poured His Spirit into all of them!

While this may be what Scripture teaches, the Christian industrial complex has *functioned* for over 1700 years with a *different* set of rules. Today's religious norms communicate that there are those qualified for ministry and those who are not. Some are trained and equipped to minister and some are not.

Eventually people believed this separation was reflective of God's value system, and the rift between clergy and laity continued to grow wider and wider. Clergy wore royal robes and were given salaries, titles, favors, and elevated positions. The message was clear: they were seen as having a 'special relationship' with God while 'ordinary' believers were viewed as ignorant of the ways of God.

Webster's defines layman as "a person who is not a priest or cleric || a person without recognized status or expert knowledge, in contrast to a professional man."[1]

While a belief in the priesthood of every believer might have been eroding before 312 A.D., Constantine codified the division between clergy and laity. He replaced Spirit-qualified leadership with a contrived, man-centered management structure. As this unscriptural division developed, more and more believers sat back and let the appointed 'leaders' take over.

This unscriptural division of clergy and laity has created what my wife calls a 'Christian caste system.' Greater deference is commonly given to those higher in the pecking order.

Modern Christian culture continues to reinforce this teaching that work is either sacred or secular. Broadly speaking, 'sacred' work is defined as any work done for the church, in the church building, or for the poor and destitute. The prevailing understanding is that "sacred work" is more valuable, more holy and more *significant*. The message (intended or otherwise) is that "ministry" is more pleasing to God, and "ministers" are the favored sons.

But God does not have favorites. We are all members of one Body. We all have something to offer. God doesn't divide us into pastors and pew sitters, ministers and nobodies. Because of His Divine Nature in us, we are all ministers and carriers of Christ. The 'spiritual' divisions we use today were not part of the culture of the early Church. Sure, the word 'ministry' exists – but not in the way we use it.

---

1. The NEW Lexicon Webster's dictionary of the English language. (1988). Lexicon Publications.

Ministry is what priests do.

Paul writes, "But to each one is given the manifestation of the Spirit [the spiritual illumination and enabling of the Holy Spirit] for the common good." (1 Cor. 12:7) and again, "Now you [collectively] are Christ's body, and individually [you are] members of it [each with his own special purpose and function]." (1 Cor. 12:27)

Every believer is a priest. A priest is responsible to represent Christ *both* in the fellowship of believers as well as in his work. Because they belong to Christ, anything a believer does can be be done as unto the LORD. The means everything they do is holy, significant and an act of worship. In God's economy, there are no sacred / secular labels!

This caste system is the enemy's ploy calculated to dismiss and disqualify the majority of believers. While this may not be stated explicitly, the "body language" of the modern church service reinforces the idea that those not "in the ministry" have little of value to offer except money or service to church-sanctioned programs. Have you ever been to a commissioning service for a carpenter or a salesman? Do we honor every occupation and person equally?

A person's employment is often considered valuable only as a means of funding the 'sacred work' of the Church. The ugly underbelly of this ideology is that it communicates that God is less interested in other vocations. Consequently, while believers might be encouraged to enter every field of work, the work itself isn't often considered to have any real "Kingdom value" except as a platform from which to evangelize the lost.

Reaching the lost is good stuff, to be sure, but it's pretty challenging if you're a farmer. Not many people in a corn field. Conversely, a lab tech's employment can be elevated one holiness level if she gives a percentage of her income to those 'in ministry.'

The emergence of this sacred-secular dichotomy has confused millions into thinking that only "church work" is holy. It implies that what everyone else does is irrelevant, unholy, insignificant, or at best secondary. Case in point: we now differentiate ministry from any other occupation.

Which is exactly what the enemy wanted.

God doesn't think that way. Scripture teaches that any work done as unto the LORD is holy. It is an act of worship. (Col. 3:23) If Jesus wanted professional and credentialed leaders, he would never have picked the ruffians he chose to be his disciples. He did not pick the religious elite.

The Kingdom is *everywhere* His people are. That was the big idea of the gospel.

Ragamuffin Priests

Our goal here is to rediscover Primal Church—a fellowship of believers that mirrors the form and function of the early church but in the modern era.

After years of study and observation, we have come to the conclusion that one of the primary reasons the early church demonstrated the power of God was because the gift of Christ was welcomed in every believer.

I'm not talking about tithing, serving in children's church, nursery, ushering, greeting, cleaning, serving on the ministry team or volunteering to park cars.

Presenting Christ in me to the people around me looks very different than maintaining a program.

Organized religion corrals believers into a type of gathering where they are not expected to bring anything of spiritual substance. While some pastors resent the lack of input from the congregants, the furniture is set up for parishioners not to participate.

Generally, there are rules: Pastors are in charge; everyone else follows. Those that try to interject interfere with the program.

Doe, my wife, describes it like this: Imagine you are invited to a pot-luck. You go through the trouble of shopping, preparing, and creating a beautiful dish designed to nourish your friends. When you arrive, the hostess greets you with a smile, takes your dish, and hides it carefully away. Then she brings out her own food (which may or may not be any better than yours) and presents that to the guests as the only option.

If that happened, we would all understand this to be rude, dishonoring, dismissive, and in desperately poor taste. Yet, we endure this exact affront week after week when the Sunday service makes no space to share our own encounter with Christ.

It's rude.

It's dishonoring.

It's dismissive.

And it's in desperately poor taste.

What's worse? It dishonors Christ. According to Scripture, my participation is **essential** for us to see the full picture of Christ. "But to **each one** is given the manifestation of the Spirit [the spiritual illumination and the enabling of the Holy Spirit] for the common good." (1 Cor. 12:7, emphasis mine)

We should be offended by the status quo. Instead, we've normalized a type of pseudo-christian interaction that contradicts the biblical mandate and model for a functioning Body of believers.

We'll know the Body is functioning effectively when our level of impact on culture starts to look more like that of the Primal Church.

The current church model restricts the expression of every believer's spiritual gift. This is like forbidding children to work but expecting them to magically become adults.

Getting older and growing up aren't the same thing.

Nothing magical happens when children turn eighteen. Discipling a child into adulthood happens primarily by show and tell. I don't tell my kids how to mow the lawn, I show them. Then I watch them do it. I create a safe place to practice and where it's okay to fail. Then I let them do it alone. Then I let them teach their younger siblings. Once this happy little circle gets going, I can sit down and sip my iced tea. I'm no longer essential to the process.

Bottom line: Children don't become contributing members of society if they never have to do hard things.

The other bottom line: our goal as parents is to raise the next generation of parents.

As believers, we won't grow if we aren't given opportunity and responsibility within the fellowship to practice hearing God and exercising our gifts. (See Eph. 4:13-16) Using our spiritual gifts requires that we take a risk. Risk strengthens our faith muscles. The modern church is full of immature believers precisely because they've not been expected to express Christ when they come together.

Jesus showed his disciples how to bring the Father's blessing (Kingdom) to earth. Then He sent them out to practice.

Simply put: Jesus *actually* expected his disciples (that now includes us) to do *everything* He had been doing.

In a Primal Church, every believer brings the intimate Presence of Christ to the fellowship. Each one serves as a priest 'for the common good' of the Body.

It is, in fact, not especially complicated. It only gets complicated when we try to imagine how this might work in the context of our current systems.

On the ground, it looks a lot more like practicing hospitality.

It looks like noticing or sensing when someone isn't doing well. It looks like really listening to what is going on in their life. It looks like being moved with compassion to pray for them right then and there. It looks like the Holy Spirit giving a word of encouragement, prophecy or wisdom simply because you stopped to love.

We've seen it.

We saw it when God healed Allen of rheumatoid arthritis because others stopped to pray for him and wash his feet. We saw it when Stacy's back was healed after a prophetic word about her marriage. We saw it when Martin, during prayer, heard that God had always wanted him – even though his earthly father never did. We saw it the day Desiree was delivered from the sweating, raging torment of demonic oppression and returned to absolute peace. We saw it when six-year-old Logan prayed for health concerns not mentioned to anyone. We saw it when Devin found people who would step over the mess of his addiction to pornography and to heal his broken heart.[1]

This is actual face-time, real heart-level interaction where everyone is seen, loved and touched. Every one of these happened in a regular old living room. There's no magic to a living room. It was simply the place where the whole Body was welcome to participate in this thing we call "fellowship with Christ."

---

1. Names have been changed.

Contrast this to your typical Sunday morning when everyone shows up with a smile (real or plastic) and gets hustled into seats for the start of the service where the same 98% always sit and listen.

A typical Sunday service does not begin to represent our highest and best opportunity to grow spiritually or to encourage one another as the writer of Hebrews admonishes. If your church programs leave you with little or no time for authentic, priestly connection as a family of believers, walk away. We only have so much time.

Don't chase the silver and lose the gold.

Choose the best over busy; the essential over what is socially acceptable.

If we aren't part of an interactive fellowship with Christ in others, you're not experiencing church.

It's not Constantine's fault.

It's not the pastor's fault.

It's not the denomination's fault.

Before God, I am responsible for my own spiritual growth and maturity.

To step away from acceptable religious activity might sound sacrilegious. It is easy to allow tradition and the passage of time to add a sacred veneer to institutions that are not, in fact, based on a Scriptural model for communion.

Please understand, our purpose is not to disqualify anyone involved in the current expression of Christianity. Neither is it our desire to vilify those who have faithfully given themselves in service. Our goal is simply to desanctify institutions and systems that have no Biblical precedent. What we have come to call "church" is actually not essential to Christianity.

Consequently, we should not be afraid to throw off the man-made tradition or the inherited prejudice of ecumenical hierarchies. Historically, these have proven to interfere with the biblical function of Christian fellowship.

The bottom line is this:

The institutions, programs and hierarchies so common today were added almost 300 years after Pentecost. These often run counter to the clear teaching of Scripture. They are not, therefore, sanctioned by God and need not be considered holy or sacrosanct.

Carry the Fire

The end goal is to pursue a level of authentic and powerful encounter with Christ in each other rarely experienced in modern churchianity.

Since every priest is essential for the Body of Christ to function effectively, we need to keep a few things straight:

1. Every believer is responsible to cultivate their own relationship with Christ.

We have one job: to keep our face and affection toward God. In the Old Testament, a primary priestly duty was to keep the altar fire burning 24/7, come wind, rain or storm. In the same way, it is our job to tend the fire of our own intimacy with Christ.

You've probably been asked, "Where do you get fed?"

This question reflects wrong thinking.

Nowhere did Jesus suggest that your spiritual journey was someone else's job. He broke ground by suggesting we interact intimately with God as our own Father. Furthermore, the invitation to remain in Christ was pointed, personal and practical. You can not and should not expect an external religious system, pastor or podcast (for example) to sustain your intimate relationship with God.

Get your own damn fork. Feed yourself!

Jesus nails this down when he said, "for [otherwise] apart from Me [that is, cut off from vital union with me] you can do nothing." (Matthew 15:5)

Every believer is a temple where Christ dwells. My connection with Him is mine to steward.

Every.

Single.

Day.

I am a priest. I tend my own fire—my affection for, and relationship with Christ. We are called disciples, not consumers. A consumer warms himself by someone else's fire. A disciple tends the fire of his own intimacy with God.

2. When we gather for fellowship, every disciple comes ready to give and receive.

If I fail to tend my personal connection to Christ, then I come to the potluck empty-handed.

This doesn't mean we have to come with a three point sermon. Please don't! We bring whatever happens to be cooking in the kitchen of our heart. Sometimes it's half-baked. Sometimes it is a word of praise or testimony or prayer. Sometimes it is an act of service as sincere as listening for what God is doing. This may only be stirred up when we gather. Every priest leans-in. The Holy Spirit does what He wants. If you don't know what this looks like, don't sweat it.

A potluck can feel like a mystery dinner, but **authentic and vulnerable sharing invites the Holy Spirit.** Remember, we don't need writing on the walls or the audible voice of God. We're not looking for hype, we're learning to love one another.

Miracles follow love.

Sure, we all face valleys, dark times, periods of brokenness and grief. If you're in that place, be vulnerable enough to share it. Even in that, I see Christ. For Christ is authentic and humble. If you have sinned, bring a confession. Through this the fellowship gets to participate in your reconciliation with Christ.

3. Honor one another.

As you honor one another, you attract the Holy Spirit. Every person carries the image of Christ, therefore, it is my privilege to welcome His Presence in each disciple who gathers around my table or living room. The children, the poor, the elderly, and the tattoo artist who loves Jesus. To do otherwise shows favoritism and disregards the plain teaching of Scripture.

We need the Spirit of God in each other like we need oxygen. Generally speaking, a group should be small enough to interact and see the many faces of Christ in the room. According to Scripture, legitimate groups can be as small as two or three and can happen anywhere Jesus is.

And Jesus is—like—everywhere.

The gifts God desires to bring to the earth are delivered through children, women and men who belong to the Father. This is how God purposes to influence our world.

4. Walk in Purity

Just as it is our job to tend the fire, it is also our responsibility to guard the gates. Our zeal for God drives us to protect what is sacred. Purity starts with ourselves and extends to our family and the people with whom we fellowship.

Whatever doesn't honor Christ – doesn't belong in my heart.

By way of example, as a father, it is also my job to guard my family and make sure Christ is honored in my home. ("As for me and my house..." Joshua 24:15)

What I don't forbid, I allow.

That includes bad attitudes, disrespect, dishonor, ingratitude, dishonesty and disobedience.

As a dad, I take a hard line here. This doesn't mean I am a perfectionist authoritarian, but I am ALWAYS disciplining my children into an understanding of what it means to honor Christ, mother, father, and siblings. Honesty, gratitude, and honor are a delight to be around. In fact, I expect honor from my children whether or not they accept Christ as their King.

When someone moves to England from another country, they are expected to drive on the left hand side of the road like everyone else. Why? They are under the governing authority of that Kingdom even if they are not a citizen of that Kingdom.

The same is true of the family of believers. We dishonor Christ in our fellowship if we allow others to dishonor Him or His children. Those who are in it for themselves (who like to drive their own agenda, hear their own voice or have all the answers) don't belong at our table. Neither do those who despise what is holy and disregard covenant. "What fellowship can light have with darkness?" (See 2 Cor. 6:14-16)

If I host a gathering of believers, then it's my job to foster an environment that doesn't grieve the Holy Spirit but provides a safe space for disciples to be vulnerable. The table is for the broken, the humble, the hungry and the repentant. Be discerning about who you invite because it is easier to go slow and cautious then it is to uninvited someone who is damaging or unhealthy for the group.

God expects spiritual fathers and mothers to protect the family culture. That's what the gift of discernment is for! Seek God. Make the hard calls. Protect the table of fellowship.

Furniture Matters

The cathedral's massive oak doors and columns tower over the entrance. A spectral silence yawns into the vestibule of stone and multi-story tapestries. Overhead, the dome draws eyes skyward where a spear of light pours through the oculus. Iconography and statuary situated on high perches look down on the lowly. Grand tiles and carved pews mark a place for commoners to sit and watch. A place to feel poor and very small.

Beyond the altar, mahogany stairs spiral to a raised pulpit. A leather-and-gold bound copy of the Holy Scriptures awaits the robed man of God. Long low tones from a pipe organ rise from the earth itself.

The beauty is formal and untouchable.

Architecture and layout set the stage either for connection or distance. The arrangement of furniture and the program all define what to expect. If I am to sit in rows looking up at a stage, then I understand myself to be part of an audience. Sure – it's practical and we all like to be able to see, but the optics are important to note. The elevated (honored) ones speak, the lower level remains quiet except for the amen corner. This does not mean that every person who speaks from a stage *thinks of themselves* as elevated. That's not the point. Furniture and position communicate a value paradigm. A few are elevated; the rest are not. The physical realm reflects a spiritual reality; the way we set our furniture mirrors what we believe.

Furniture reveals what we honor. It communicates rank, legitimacy, significance, or intimacy. Be it intentional or by happenstance, furniture helps to define or confine the function of a setting. A friend of mine used to say, "Everything communicates."

As Viola and Barna aptly note, "the [church] building is an architectural denial of the priesthood of all believers."[1]

Conversely, a warm kitchen with the smell of home-baked bread feels welcoming, intimate and comfortable.

When we walk into our friends' house, we're first greeted by their dog whose entire back-end wags with delight. Our friends wrap us in hugs. Dinner smells divine, and we add our dish to the table. The front door opens as more people pour in. Laughter ensues. We coalesce at the kitchen island in twos and threes or sit in the living room. We share our food, our lives, our stories, our failures and our triumphs. There's no minimum group size to authenticate fellowship. Two or three actually qualifies. Don't underestimate the power of a small group gathered in His name!

We treasure Christ in each other.

We pray for each other. We laugh hard. We cry sometimes. We are authentic, flexible, phone-free, and tuned in to each other and to

---

1. Viola, F., & Barna, G. (2012). *Pagan Christianity? : exploring the roots of our church practices.* Barna.

what God is doing. As we look for Him in one another, the treasuries of the King are opened to His family.

This reflects the scriptural model for church.

Practically speaking, a living room layout puts everyone in the front-row. There's no hiding. no performing. No back row. No stage. No program. No set plan, pattern or agenda. We can intentionally welcome the Holy Spirit anywhere "two or three are gathered." (Matt. 18:20) Living rooms equalize people. Here everyone has merit, everyone has something to offer, everyone is an important member of the family.

Please understand, I'm not suggesting we *never* meet as a large group. I *am* suggesting that the modern church-experience isn't actually "church" according to the New Testament. In a typical service today, furniture, platform, pastor and program all serve as a bottleneck to encountering the Presence of Christ in each other. The 'normal' Sunday service bypasses what the Holy Spirit wants to give His Bride.

Consequently, we cannot remain in the current model without doing damage to God's redemptive plan for the earth. A large meeting of believers might be exciting, but it doesn't come close to the type of gathering Paul describes as *essential* to our spiritual growth and maturity.

In short, a meeting of Christians does not equal the fellowship of believers any more than going to a Christian concert, play or movie. Remember, furniture (by itself) isn't the problem.

We first need a paradigm reset.

Simply moving the traditional Sunday service into a house does not deal with the root problem. Why? Because we have a culture that idolizes leaders, their gifts and their charisma. Because our culture also idolizes comfort and consumerism, we happily abdicate our priestly responsibility to others.

Scriptural Model

Christ has always purposed to be known in and through *every* believer in order to bless *all* creation. When the Holy Spirit revealed Himself through the early church, entire regions were transformed. What was normal for church then, we now call revival.

In fact, the way God works in revival is important to note.

Revival activates the Scriptural model of fellowship as any and every believer becomes a conduit through which the Spirit might move. Even the unlikely participate.

Every revival started with a few who longed for Christ to draw near. In answer to their desire, the Spirit came. For a while, He was the center of attention. In Wales, for example, the Spirit orchestrated testimonies, songs, and the flow anywhere His people got together. The result was the great unleashing of a royal priesthood. According to the observers, the primary fruit of Welsh revival was the restoration of the family altar. Fathers and mothers would lead their own families into fellowship with each other and Christ.[1] While the expression of Christ in every believer may seem wild or unpredictable to our modern sensibilities, it was essential to the effective function of the early church.

Now when revival comes, we inevitably drift back to the familiar tradition of man-directed services, building-centered meetings, agendas and professional leadership. At first, for example, the Azusa revival remained completely under the direction of God. While it was without program, it was not without order. But eventually it suffered the same fate as every other revival.[2]

While we may experience temporary moves of God, our operating system has never shifted from the patterns codified under Constantine. The inertia of tradition slowly and relentlessly quenches the Holy Spirit until He withdraws like a wounded Lover. This pattern is so often repeated that we don't expect revivals to last!

If, in an effort to remain 'orderly', we don't honor the expression of Christ in every believer, then we disobey Scripture. The Holy Spirit does not take direction from men.

In countries where being a Christian is illegal, believers are forced into hiding and, in their desperation, learn to minister to each other. My son, Isaiah, remarked that he's heard some suggest we should welcome persecution because the church commonly explodes during times of suffering. But, he said, the reason the church grew wasn't because of persecution but simply because the persecution forced the church back into a form that reflected the scriptural

---

1. S.B. Shaw. (1905). *The Great Revival in Wales*. S.B. Shaw Publisher.

2. Bartleman, F. (1980). *Azusa Street*. Logos International. (Original work published 1925)

model for fellowship! The net result: real spiritual growth and a vibrant church.

This is a core truth from Scripture: every spiritual gift expressed in each person is a facet of His Christ's character by which he wants to be made known.

We aren't the first people to see this. According to Hyatt, "In reaction to the ecclesiastical system of Roman Catholicism, the Anabaptists rejected a hierarchical structure of leadership and emphasized that ministry was the responsibility of the entire congregation.[...] The primary reason given for not attending the state churches is that **those institutions did not allow the members of the congregation to exercise spiritual gifts according to 'the Christian order as taught in the gospel or the Word of God in 1 Corinthians 14.**'[...] The author of the document chides [Martin] Luther and Zwingli, accusing them of transgressing their own original teaching and of impeding 'the rivers of living water by not allowing the free exercise of spiritual gifts in their congregations.'" (p. 80, emphasis mine)

Hyatt notes that when the Anabaptists pulled away from the state run churches and began to look to each other as priests, they experienced an outpouring of the Holy Spirit reminiscent of Pentecost! (p. 79)

It cost many of them their lives.

Today we sit in the lap of their sacrifice, yet few are willing to follow their lead. Frank Bartleman writes, "It is like death to break away from that which has become a very part of our religious being. Tradition becomes as binding upon us as the word of God itself, and has become accepted as the same. And yet, how much tradition has been proven all wrong Scripturally" (p. 94).[3]

Our goal must always be to peel off the false veneer of spirituality and get down to the essentials of communion with Christ in each other. We must delegitimize traditions and forms that (at worst) stand opposed to the Spirit of Christ or (at best) interfere with the free function and expression of the priesthood of believers.

Christ calls His people to throw off anything that stands opposed to His multi-faceted expression on the earth. (Heb. 12:1)

While institutions, buildings, programs and positions often get in the way, **what remains most important is learning how to *be* with each other as Christ intended**. Being fully present is so much more than putting away our phones and sitting in a circle. Without authenticity, fellowship is merely a play of shadow puppets. Christ is not visible in my pretender, my imposter or my clown. All of these are baskets under which we hide the light of Christ.

Let's take a look at a few key passages referencing the Scriptural model for fellowship:

1 Corinthians 14:26

"What then is *the right course*, believers? When you meet together, **each one** has a psalm, a teaching, a revelation (disclosure of special knowledge), a tongue, *or* an interpretation." (Boldface mine; see also Eph. 5:19-21)

Ephesians 4:16

"From Him the whole body [the church, in all its various parts], joined and knitted *firmly* together **by what every joint supplies,**

---

3. Bartleman, F. (1980). Azusa Street. Logos International.

when each part is working properly causes the body to grow and mature, building itself up in [unselfish] love." (Boldface mine)

Ephesians 3:10

"So now through the church the multifaceted wisdom of God [in all its countless aspects] might now be made known [revealing the mystery] to the [angelic] rulers and authorities in the heavenly places."

Hebrews 10:24-25

"And let us consider [thoughtfully] how we may **encourage one another** to love and to do good deeds." (boldface mine)

1 Corinthians 14:31

"For [in this way] you can **all** prophesy **one by one**, so that everyone may be instructed and everyone may be encouraged." (Boldface mine)

Colossians 3:16

Paul instructs all believers (remember, this wasn't written for pastors) in Colossae, "Let the [spoken] word of Christ have its home within you [dwelling in your heart and mind-permeating every aspect of your being] **as you teach [spiritual things] and admonish and train one another...**" (Boldface mine)

Mark 7:7-9

In the Gospel of Mark, Jesus said, "'THEY WORSHIP ME IN VAIN, [their worship is meaningless and worthless, a pretense], TEACHING THE PRECEPTS OF MEN AS DOCTRINES [**giving their traditions equal weight with the Scriptures**].' You disregard and neglect the commandment of God and cling [faithfully] to the tradition of men.' He was also saying to them, '**You are experts at setting aside and nullifying the commandment of God in order to keep your [man-made] tradition and regulations.**'" (Boldface mine)

What happened?

Since Constantine, religious culture has defended—sometimes militantly—traditions that dishonor the expression of Christ in the Body. We label our Sunday services "church" when, in fact, they do not align with a Scriptural definition of fellowship. Clinging tenaciously to tradition, we maintain that attending a weekly program is a key expression of faith.

What must we do?

Return to the biblical model of fellowship—where the primary purpose is Christ being expressed through every believer.

Prophet's Reward

In Matthew 10, Jesus used a story from the Old Testament to highlight a spiritual principle.

If we want to receive a delivery then we'd better welcome those carrying the packages.

In this context, the disciples were probably feeling a lot of pressure because He had just told them to go out and heal people. If I were among them, I would have raised my hand, too. "Um, Jesus, exactly how are we going to do something we can't do?"

Jesus told his disciples, "He who receives and welcomes you receives Me, and he who receives Me receives Him who sent Me. He who receives and welcomes a prophet because he is a prophet will receive a prophet's reward; and he who receives a righteous (honorable) man because he is a righteous man will receive a righteous man's reward." (Matt. 10:40-41)

Jesus said even those who welcome His children would receive the reward they carried. (Matt. 10:42)

In short, Jesus was reminding the disciples that they were in the delivery business. Anyone who welcomed them would receive the reward (gift) they were carrying from the King.

Other people's honor activates the King's delivery system.

In the Old Testament, those who hosted the prophets Elijah and Elisha received a blessing specific to their need: a miracle of conception, the resurrection of the dead or the sustaining provision of food during famine. (See 1 Kings 17; 2 Kings 4:8) The women mentioned in connection with these miracles would not have received this "special delivery" from Heaven if they had not welcomed the one who brought it.

Their hospitality opened a door for the supernatural gift of God to be intimately expressed.

In the same way, if we want to receive what God has for us, then we must welcome the Spirit of God in each other.

If the King sends me a gift and I ignore his delivery boy, I will not get the gift. And I will dishonor the King.

If our meeting restricts the participation of believers, then we restrict our access to God's blessing of connection, healing, encouragement, deliverance and family. While it is true that the Spirit of God can 'fall on us,' Scripture teaches the primary way we are to interact with the Spirit of God is not through worship or teaching, but *through other believers.*

I am not discounting the good things that happen on a Sunday, (I hope good things do happen in your Sunday service!) but there is much more available to us! Let's not be satisfied looking at the menu and miss out on communion with Christ.

Paul is clear on this point: Every believer is a part. Every part matters. Our gifts were designed first and foremost to edify the Body of Christ. The primary reason we meet together is so that we can build each other up with the gifts we bring. Either we function as a whole — and by so doing experience the fullness of Christ — or we shut down parts of the body and fall into dysfunction. (Eph. 4:14-16; 1 Cor. 12:14-26)

An example of this principle is found in 1 Samuel 17. David knew he had legal authority to evict Goliath because Goliath was encroaching on God's promise to Israel. David carried God's authority to defeat the giant, but he needed someone to make space for him to engage. Even though his own brothers scorned him, Saul took David seriously and authorized him to fight Goliath. The king's willingness to honor what David had to offer gave all Israel access to their breakthrough moment!

The current church industry honors only the few ("clergy") and disqualifies—verbally or non-verbally—the rest of the priesthood ("laity") every time we get together. As a result, the corporate body does not have access to the full blessing of Christ. The multi-faceted gifts of the Holy Spirit were not given to maintain programs, but for us to release breakthrough and blessing to each other.

The gifts of Christ are integral to our time of fellowship. The point of a Sunday service is not to get charged up, so we can share our gifts with the world. While we are created to carry the influence of Christ into everything we do, the fundamental purpose of our spiritual gifts is for the blessing and edification of fellow believers.

That is the primary purpose of meeting together.

The fact that open participation won't work in the current framework does not disqualify the Scripture, it disqualifies our traditions.

When we don't honor the Holy Spirit in fellow believers, we become increasingly disconnected from Christ. In order to bring the full expression of the government of God to this realm, the Body of Christ must remain connected to Christ our Head.

Without the full ministry of the Holy Spirit, we fail to mature. Without maturity we cannot fulfill our destiny.

The travesty here is twofold:

The lesser travesty: we dishonor believers by ignoring what they bring to the Body. (see 1 Corinthians 12)

The greater travesty: we grieve the Holy Spirit by ignoring His Presence in them.

God has enormous treasure stored up for the earth. Most of it sits idle in a warehouse because the carriers have so often been ignored that they don't bother to show up for work anymore. The tradition and program are so familiar that we don't even feel the dishonor of being silenced.

When we teach this paradigm shift, I sometimes suggest we receive believers into our home with the question, "What do you have for me?" It might sound silly or a little selfish, but it's simply a reminder that other believers are vital to our spiritual growth.

It reminds me that others depend on my connection with Christ.

"But to each one is given the manifestation of the Spirit [the spiritual illumination and the enabling of the Holy Spirit] for the common good." (1 Corinthians 12:7)

If we don't welcome Christ in each other, why should we be surprised when our normal doesn't include seeing the sick healed, the demoniac delivered, the dead raised and those in bondage set free?

Leadership

When we read the Bible, we often superimpose our traditions or preconceptions onto them. Unfortunately, the grid of traditional assumptions and rigid thinking has caused us to read systems and structures into Scripture that didn't exist when it was written.

Hierarchies, denominations, programs, and professional qualifications (for example) *did not exist* in the New Testament.

Leadership, however, *is* Scriptural and *just as necessary as every other gift God gave the Body*. When we pull back the drapery of tradition and broken paradigms, we begin to see leadership framed out in a completely different light.

Healthy Leadership

Paul tells us that leaders are recognized by:
- how they lead their family
- their speech, life, love, faith, hope and purity
- their care, and love for the Body of Christ
- a long faithful walk with God
- humility and service

The gifts of leadership are given to serve the body—not to manage budgets, programs or meetings. Leaders keep Christ at the center. If a body of believers centers around a person, then it is dysfunctional. Primal Church leaders bless and release others in their gifting. Leaders reproduce themselves. Spiritual fathers and mothers raise up spiritual fathers and mothers. They create space to learn, grow, fail, and try again. Leaders are not threatened by other leaders. They are not jealous, withholding or controlling. They don't demand recognition, title, or compensation.

Notice: Primal Church leaders are not qualified by charisma, miracles, giftedness, popularity, or their ability to hold other people's attention.

A leader's primary purpose is to create spiritual families centered around Christ. Leaders make sure the fellowship table is reserved for disciples. These healthy mothers and fathers have dealt with their own idolatries of religion, fear of man, or the love of significance. They are, therefore, qualified to guard the gates against detractors, manipulators, networkers and charlatans. Leaders are students of the Word and friends of God. Leaders set the parameter and culture for the family of God.

They are gifted to keep the main thing the main thing.

True leaders won't prioritize peace over purity; they are not afraid of confrontation. Because they walk in love, a mature leader will forbid discrimination, dishonor and favoritism. This is one of the ways they protect the flock and provide a spiritual covering.

New Testament leaders were often older men and women devoted to Christ. The leadership *gifts* mentioned in Ephesians and elsewhere (apostle, prophet, teacher, evangelist, shepherd) were never intended to be positions or employment. (Remember, Constantine institutionalized that idea.) Those gifts were never meant to occupy the top tier of an org chart. Spiritual fathers and mothers were honored but not elevated. In the primal church there was no paid access. The way of Jesus does not include titles, salaries, special robes, stages, or platforms.

Leaders clean kitchens, tend wounds, wash feet, and honor the Spirit of God in everyone. They may not stand out, but we'd notice if they were missing. It is right to honor those who are spiritually mature, faithful and connected to the Holy Spirit. But we can honor without centering around them. The center point of our table is always Christ.

When Paul told Titus to appoint elders in every city (See Titus 1:5), he wasn't asking Titus to appoint central figures around which the church should gather. True elders/leaders were simply mature fathers and mothers who took responsibility for the growth of believers in their region.

Our spiritual gifts are not job titles, neither are they an identity. Spiritual gifts simply define the nature of our service in the fellowship of believers. Godly leaders don't get people to follow them—they lead people to follow Christ.

Leadership is not a job or a position. It is a gift of the Holy Spirit and is often the fruit of hiddenness, long endurance, and faithfulness despite suffering.

Those rooted and grounded in the love of God don't seek to elevate themselves. The humble, who serve the Body out of love, don't need to be significant in the eyes of man. Servanthood comes from a heart secure in God's love.

When leaders need the love and recognition of people, it is not service—it is manipulation.

Unhealthy Leaders

Jesus pointedly called out the Scribes and Pharisees for trying to distinguish themselves above others. "But do not be called Rabbi (Teacher); for One is your Teacher, and **you are all [equally] broth-**

ers. Do not call *anyone* on earth [who guides you spiritually] your father; for One is your Father, He who is in heaven. Do not *let yourselves* be called leaders *or* teachers; for One is your Leader (Teacher), the Christ. But the greatest among you will be your servant." (Matt. 23:8-11, boldface mine)

The current role of pastor can set the stage—literally and figuratively—for dysfunction.

Because of religious strongholds and longheld traditions, pastors are often considered holy, elevated, significant and important. The furniture, the stage, and the emotive elements folded into the regular Sunday meeting all enforce this persona. It's a set-up for idolatry. Women—who compare their husbands to a pastor—fall into spiritual adultery or crippling criticism of their husbands. Unable to compete, men often abdicate responsibility for the spiritual growth of their family to the pastor.

Pastors are hired to "feed" the people, counsel in crisis, preach, pray, manage church events, handle all the administrative elements related to finances – including salaries, benefits, outreach and compassion ministries, oversee additional staff, confront the wayward, mentor, marry, bury, and baptize. They are also supposed to be available when everyone else isn't working (think evenings and weekends). They are expected to pony up whenever someone in their congregation has a personal, relational, spiritual or health crisis. Pastors are expected to please everyone—and everyone feels entitled to their time. After all, they pay the pastor's salary, right?

Then, pastors are left to grovel for congregational participation where extra help is needed—and it's always needed. They can end up frustrated, disappointed or bitter at the very people they're supposed to care for.

Because pastors are expected to set the gold standard for personal holiness, they are subjected to a fishbowl existence where every member of their family is openly scrutinized, vilified, or elevated. Slander, gossip or congregational "concerns" works like an ever-present abrasive on their soul. They have usually faced betrayal of the worst kind. The marriage failure and burn-out rates for pastors are obscene. Because it is unsafe to be vulnerable with anyone, pastors often lead a terrifyingly isolated and siloed existence.

It is, quite frankly, a perfect set-up for loneliness, burnout, failed marriage, and moral failure—or for bitterness, fear and control.

Abusive Leaders

Our western culture idolizes movie stars, athletes, and musicians. The Christian industrial complex keeps pace by idolizing 'anointed' speakers, evangelists, missionaries, and worship leaders. Personality cults are a perversion of leadership. This is where a person is considered (or considers himself) central to what God is doing. In these situations, people considered 'essential personnel' to that system are often excused of sexual abuse, financial misconduct, bullying, and fraud.

Platforms, promotion and marketing can hide abusive leaders. These leaders might have elder or advisory boards, but those elders carry no real authority. These yes-men get selected because they are successful, well connected or wealthy.

Abusive church leaders or their wives can be identified by the presence of bullying, jealousy, slander, flattery, manipulation, spiritual authoritarianism, intimidation, control, partiality, suppression of gifts, mockery, gas-lighting, lies, and a lack of transparency. What may appear to be staggering success can easily run alongside a lack of financial integrity, sexual abuse, or disregard for women in abusive or toxic marriages.

Many abusive leaders today use favoritism and spiritual discrimination as tools to maintain control under the guise of 'keeping order,' 'protecting the flock' or 'preserving sound doctrine.'

Not all of the above need to be present to constitute spiritual abuse. The list can (and does) get a lot uglier.

If you find yourself in a place like this, don't walk away.

Run.

You'll be glad you did.

Want more? Visit primalchurch.org for the free download on **Religious Elitism.**

Section III
The Mission

THE MISSION

In order to train appropriately, we first need to understand exactly why we're here!

At one time, I worked with a consulting company. One of our clients was an organization composed of former Special Forces operatives. It was probably the only meeting I've attended where concealed weapons outnumbered people, three to one. These men had seen action all over the world, and most of it they couldn't talk about. In their line of work, they had to show up like ghosts, complete their mission, and disappear before daybreak.

It's not an easy line of work; they endured years of grueling, focused, and intense training. They mastered the capacity to work as a team under deplorable conditions. They hardened their bodies, toughened their minds, and learned types of warcraft I've never heard of.

If you have a friend stuck in the middle of a bloody conflict in the African bush, these are the guys you'd want to call.

Why? Because they are a no-nonsense, get-shit-done, badass company of exceptional soldiers with a specific skill set that's pretty hard to locate on LinkedIn. Their training perfectly suits their mission.

In the same way, we must understand the nature of our mission, or we might end up in a basket-weaving class when we should be sky-diving—or a pottery class when we need parkour.

Please understand, I'm not against the arts and I'm not in favor of sky-diving.

The point is, **our understanding of the mission determines the focus of our discipleship**.

We are commissioned to go into all the world and make disciples, right? So, let's drill down and make sure our discipleship manual actually lines up with the mission brief.

Some would say our mission is simply to get people saved so they can spend eternity with God.

Actually, that is not correct. In fact, the great fallacy of our age is that the salvation of souls is the mission of the Church.

Salvation is only *part* of the gospel.

The enemy has propogated the idea that God's 'master plan' is all about how-not-to-go-to-hell-when-you-die. In dumbing down the good news to a retirement package, the enemy has kept the Church endlessly pre-occupied with the wrong thing.

A Paradise or Hell focused "gospel" always results in a bungled mission. We have beautiful buildings, moving sermons and top-shelf worship leaders. We have state-of-the-art equipment and international audiences. We have settled for endless sermons to crowds of pew-sitting, bum-scratching believers anxiously waiting for Jesus to rescue them before the planet self-destructs.

Meanwhile, the country's media and educational systems teach no absolute values. Injustice prevails in our government and courts. Most families are broken and divided. Our food, water, and air are poisoned. Disease abounds. Creation groans under the rebellion of man all while we're busy singing 'I'll Fly Away.'

My son, Isaiah, described it this way: "Christians tend to look at these issues and say, 'Well these are just the trials Jesus talked about,' and never bother trying to fix it. They think a broken world is inevitable."

According to Scripture, all creation is waiting to be redeemed from oppression, not left to rot. (Rom. 8:19) First and foremost, we are saved to restore our intimacy with the Father, secondly we are saved to carry His influence into all creation.

A paradise-focused Church poses no threat to the enemy's plan to ruin humanity and the Earth.

Paradise is definitely a perk, but it's not the *point*.

Our mission is to bring the government and blessing of God *to this world*. Jesus taught His disciples to pray, "On earth as it is in heaven." (Matt. 6:10) The Gospel is good news for now, not just good news for later.

Turns out, our mission has always been the same.

The Beginning

God created two realms: Heaven and Earth.

We were fashioned after God both in form and function. God created Mankind to exercise His authority on Earth. We look like God and are filled with the Spirit of God so that we might bless the earth with God.

Before the fall, Adam's job was an overflow of his relationship with the Creator. Man was created for the express purpose of caring for the earth—to bless and steward and rule effectively. The created world was *specifically designed* to thrive under righteous leadership.

God created mankind to function in a life-giving and symbiotic relationship with all creation. To do this, He breathed His very own nature into man. The Breath of God in mankind is the very essence of what holds all things together. Christ is, according to Scripture, "the controlling, cohesive force of the universe." (Col. 1:17)

The Rebellion

As His image bearers, humanity was designed to represent God to all creation. God entrusted creation to mankind and instructed us to care for it on His behalf. Since God deeded Earth to mankind, we alone held the *legal* right to give away that title.

That is precisely why the enemy seduced Adam and Eve into rebellion. The only way satan could set up his throne in this realm was by getting Earth's title deed from man. So he drew Adam and Eve into deception. When Adam and Eve rebelled against God, they abdicated their authority and forfeited land title to the enemy.

We need to be clear: The enemy didn't defeat God and take God's throne on Earth. He deceived Adam and Eve and took took away their right to rule. "Do you not know...You are the slaves of the one you obey." (Rom. 6:16) The enemy needed man to give him the title in order to have permission to work here.

Christ's death and resurrection returned our Adamic authority to govern, so that we might bring Earth back under a life-giving administration.

That's why Jesus said, the Kingdom (Goverment) of Heaven is *at hand*. (Matt. 4:17)

According to the Apostle Paul, "[even the whole] creation [all nature] waits eagerly for the children of God to be revealed...in hope that creation itself will also be freed from its bondage to decay [and gain entrance] into the glorious freedom of the children of God." (Rom. 8:19, 20b-21)

Is Creation waiting for God?

No.

Creation is waiting for you.

The Master's Plan

Ever since man fell, the Master's plan to redeem and restore all creation has been underway.

Just as all creation was subjected to the curse because of the fall of man, so the redemption of all creation can come through one man (Christ). The Sacrifice of Christ (the second Adam) made it possible for our relationship with God to be restored.

Repentance reconnects us to the "power-grid" of Heaven. As sin brought destruction and ruin to mankind and the earth, so when Christ restored our connection to the Healer and Redeemer, we got our authority back. God purposed first to restore our intimate connection to Him and then, by the extension of His influence in us, to heal the earth.

Remember, "Kingdom" doesn't mean Heaven. The coming of God's Kingdom means we extend God's rule and authority to Earth. We exercise that authority as His regents.

Christ's sacrifice reinstated the legal right and capacity to pursue the King's vision for everything on the earth. Jesus did not only come to rescue us from hell but to restore us to the authority and influence Adam had before the rebellion.

Return to Eden

God created Adam and Eve specifically to care for the earth.

The current missional standard for the modern church is (usually) getting people saved and 'connected' to a local church program. But where the modern goal has been to keep people out of hell, God's goal has (always) been to bring complete reformation to *every part* of creation.

Some wait for revival and miracles to bring a quick fix; others wait for the rapture. But while we've been waiting for God to redeem this mess, He been waiting for us.

We need to up our game and get with His program!

I didn't make this up. It's all in The Book.

According to Scripture, God's endgame is:

"And the wolf will dwell with the lamb [...] They will not hurt or destroy on all My holy mountain." (Isa. 11:6-9)

"And all the hills shall melt [that is, **everything that was once barren will overflow** with streams of blessing]." (Amos 9:13-16, emphasis mine)

"Nation shall not lift up sword against nation, **nor shall they ever again train for war**." (Micah 4:1-5, emphasis mine)

"**The earth** shall be filled with the knowledge of the glory of the LORD, as the waters cover the sea." (Hab. 2:14, emphasis mine)

"Nation will not lift up sword against nation, and never again will they learn war." (Isa. 2:4)

God-inspired art and industry. (Ex. 31: 3-5)

Raising the dead. Healing the blind, sick and lame. (John 14:12)

As the prophet Isaiah foretold, "For to us a Child shall be born, to us a Son shall be given; And the government shall be upon His shoulder, [and] *There shall be no end to the increase of His government and of peace.*" (Isa. 9:6-7a, emphasis mine)

We are not "saved" to escape the earth but to bless it. When we live from the wonder of God's intimate friendship, death starts working backwards (to borrow a line from C.S. Lewis). The rebellion of man wounded creation; the reconciliation of man empowers us to heal it.

To heal the Earth is the job description. Paradise is the benefit package. We'd do well not to confuse the two.

Tikkun Olam

Generally speaking, Christians live like this world is to be survived.

Counter to that, the idea of repairing the world is baked into Jewish culture. Tikkun Olam is a Hebrew phrase that means "repairing the world." This idea encourages us to see everything we do here (family, community, work, innovation) as important. Small wonder that a huge percentage of earth-shaking breakthroughs and innovations have come from Jews.

Tikkun Olam is a kingdom mindset that says (for example) *good* business has to be good for me *and* you or it's not really good for me. This stands opposed to our prevailing, self-centered culture.

The solutions to every problem on earth are planted in the hearts of men and women. The passion of our heart is often a clue to what God wants to do on the earth. Why? Because God has chosen to partner with humanity to heal the earth.

George Washington Carver cared about the peanut.

Archimedes loved math and science.

The Wright brothers wanted to fly.

John and Abigail Adams had a desire to establish godly government.

Milton Hershey loved chocolate.

Thank God they pursued their passions!

The Paradise gospel often devalues what it considers to have no eternal significance. The allure of significance connected to 'church' work, seduces some believers away from what they are created to do. They are duped into believing the 'ministry' is more noble than a 'secular' job.

Serving the industry of church and serving God are not equivalent. Every time a disciple denies the passions of his heart (calling them selfish) to serve church programs, God's redemptive plan on Earth is suppressed.

Joseph Lister was born into a Quaker family that encouraged the study of science. His father perfected the microscope and made significant improvements to the instrument through the course of his life. As a result of his father's innovations, when Joseph decided to pursue the path of medicine, he took a microscope with him — an instrument which was uncommon in the field of medicine at that time.

Lister attended the University College of London. In the course of his study, he almost abandoned medicine for work in the church. He was eventually persuaded to stay the course.

It's a good thing he did.

Today, hospitals are a place to go for help. In Lister's day, hospitals were known as places to die. Mortality rates after major surgeries hovered around forty percent.

Through that microscope his father perfected, Joseph Lister recognized evidence of infection being transferred from one patient to another through the unwashed hands and the blood smeared aprons of the doctors. Lister saw the need for medical personnel to sanitize hands, clothes, bandages, and instruments between patients. He pioneered the antiseptic process that we now take for granted.

Initially, Lister's work was vehemently mocked by the medical establishment. But he persisted, and once his methods were implemented, mortality rates in some wards dropped to less than three percent![1]

Today, Joseph Lister is considered the father of modern surgery.

If we preach the gospel of salvation and never address what is broken in creation, we miss the mission of Christ. (Mk 16:15) God purposes to demonstrate his wisdom and care through every system on earth.

What is happening out there—in culture, industry, technology, agriculture, design, fashion, family, education—is the true litmus test for the quality of our discipleship and the best indicator of the missional success of the church.

The King needs representatives in every walk of life, and—in case you haven't caught on yet—that's exactly how God planned it. Every believer is his priest—men, women and children. First to each other, then to all creation.

Ditch diggers, lab techs, schoolteachers, mathematicians, cowboys, actors, police, farmers, mechanics, pilots, skippers and even the guys who work with extrusion molding, janitors, mothers and fathers, the intellectual and the simple, the beautiful and the homely.

Adam gardened.

Bezalel and Oholiab were filled with the Spirit to be artisans and craftsmen. (Exodus 35:30-35)

Joseph was a project manager.

---

1. Fitzharris, L. (2017). *The Butchering Art*. Penguin UK.

Nehemiah was the quality control manager for the royal liquor board.

Amos watched sheep.

Jesus built stuff.

God loves to do life with us. He wants to be involved in every detail of our work, our families, our industries, and our play. He has unlimited resources, innovation, and expertise to share!

As we spend time in fellowship with Christ in each other, we become more like Him and thereby manifest His kingdom all around us. Intimacy with God restores our capacity to influence this realm.

Rapture?

Many Bible schools today promote an eschatology out of step with what Jesus taught. While a comprehensive discussion of rapture is beyond the scope of this work, my goal is to point out the obvious. A direct and honest reading of Scripture shows the wicked will be removed from the earth while the righteous remain.

What would be the point of God's glory overspreading the earth if this earth doesn't really matter?

In the mid 1800's, John Nelson Darby introduced a new end-times teaching. Darby proposed that unrestrained evil will eventually overtake the world and believers will be raptured to Heaven. If you're a pre-tribber, you get to skip the worst of it. If you're a post-tribber, sorry, you'll have to endure the horror.

Two thousand years ago Jesus said His kingdom was near at hand. (Matt. 4:17) (Kingdom is not synonymous with Heaven.) Keep in mind that there is no sin in heaven. In Jesus' own words, "The Son of Man will send out His angels, and they will gather **out of His Kingdom** all things that offend [those things by which people are led into sin], and all who practice evil [leading others into sin], and will throw them into the furnace of fire [...] then THE RIGHTEOUS [those who seek the will of God] WILL SHINE FORTH [radiating the new life] like the sun in the Kingdom of their Father." (Matt. 13:41-42, boldface mine)

God is not going to send out angels to rescue the righteous from a corrupted world.

Psalm 37 reads, "For those who do evil will be cut off, But those who wait for the LORD, they will inherit the land. For yet a little while and the wicked one will be gone [forever]; Though you look carefully where he used to be, he will not be [found]. But the humble will [at last] inherit the land and will delight themselves in abundant prosperity and peace." (v. 9-11) David's psalm remains a prophetic promise.

Jesus taught His disciples to pray (*and expect*) that the will (or government) of the Father would manifest here on earth, even as it manifests in Heaven. (Matt. 6:10; Luke 11:2) Why would Jesus encourage His disciples to ask for something He had no intention of bringing to pass? He already knew the will of the Father. The will of the Father is to make Earth look like Heaven.

We are told by Isaiah that when Messiah comes, His governmental influence and peace on the earth would *always* increase (not decay or be overwhelmed by demonic zombies). "There shall be no end to the increase of His government and of peace..." (See Isa. 9:6-7)

Paul writes that just as all creation was subjected to the fall of man, so mankind and the earth will be redeemed by the blood of Christ. It's our job to restore the earth, not wait around to be rescued out of spiraling chaos. (Rom. 8:20-21; Isa. 58:12)

Paul told us, "Yet in all these things we are **more than conquerors *and* gain an overwhelming victory** through Him who loved us [so much that He died for us]." (Rom. 8:37, boldface mine) Why would Paul refer to us as conquerors if we are going to be overcome by evil?

God's plan has always been to heal the earth! That's what made the gospel such good news.

I'll still drink tea with you if you buy into Darby's theory, but when that rapture happens, I plan to stick around.

The enemy happily promoted Darby's rapture theory because satan isn't *primarily* worried about people going to heaven. He is worried about losing influence here.

The enemy's goal has always been to get believers to abdicate their role in family, government, culture, media, education, entertainment and the arts. Why? He still wants to exercise an authority on earth that was intended for man. Not much has changed. He wants to keep our focus on the afterlife. Where we abdicate, he fills the vacuum.

Sadly, it's working. The (new) rapture theory significantly shifted the mission of the Church. Instead of being God's rescue plan for Earth, believers are waiting to be rescued.

After all, Jesus is coming soon! Get 'em saved! Do it quick. The world's on fire! There's nothing like a good rapture story to put the hurry-up on getting saved. This manipulative tactic leads to fear-based conversions. Discipleship is reduced to teaching new believers how to lead others through the sinner's prayer—a prayer which Jesus never used, nor taught his disciples. We've become obsessed with evangelism and disregarded our full mission!

What's the fruit of Darby's theory?

There's no point in restoring an earth that is about to be annihilated.

It destroys any hope in God's good plans to prosper us. (Jer. 29:11)

It predisposes believers to hoard, save and protect themselves rather than love others.

It fosters a fatalistic outlook on life.

Darby's rapture theory is a market multiplier for the doomsday industry. It becomes perfectly acceptable for Christians to stock their bomb shelters with guns, bottled water, split peas, and MRE's. You might find these preppers with a "Jesus Saves!" bumper sticker and blasting the Animals' song "We gotta get out of this place."

The net result of Darby's teaching is a church system obsessed with the afterlife and disengaged from the primary mission of the gospel—the reconciliation of all the Earth.

SECTION IV
Purity & Authority

Intimacy and Influence

Since the beginning, our ability to extend the influence of God's Kingdom has been connected to personal and corporate purity. In fact, the connection between purity and dominion (extending God's blessing) is the prevailing theme from Genesis to Malachi.

Purity is, quite simply, the quality of my trust in God.

When I trust in anything else, I'm led into compromise, torment and captivity.

For example, if—even though I am saved—I believe God will not take care of me, then I will live like I have to take care of myself. That leads to compromises like not giving generously to those in need. It will lead to torment like fear, anxiety, stress, figuring it all out, and worry. And the fear that God won't take care of me could lead to captivity like workaholism or alcohol abuse. As Winkey Pratney once said, "we are punished by our sins, not for them."

God gave the Israelites legal title to the Promise Land. However, idolatry (placing trust in other gods) compromised their right to rule and opened a way for enemy torment and captivity. The Israelites held onto their authority and national security only as long as they stayed faithful to the LORD, trusting Him alone for protection, provision and blessing.

The enemy's strategy is illustrated in the story of Balaam. (See Num. 22-25; Hos. 9:10; Rev. 2:14) The leaders of Moab and Midian—when threatened by the advancing Israelites—asked Balaam to curse God's people. God would not allow Balaam to do that, so Balaam found another way to undermine Israel's authority. He instructed the Midianite elders to send their daughters to entice the Israelite men into worshiping their demon gods. (Sex was part of their ritual worship.)

It worked: Some Israelites joined the Midianites in their ceremonies. As a result of Israel's spiritual prostitution, they gave the enemy access to steal, kill, and destroy their lives, families and property. Through their compromise (worshiping another god), the Israelites relinquished their God-given authority to the enemy. As a result, the enemy was empowered to steal, kill, and destroy.

First century Jews saw the effects of idolatry everywhere. People were sick, demonized and dying. Israel was oppressed by a ruthless Roman government.

Then Jesus came along echoing the words of Old Testament prophets and John the Baptist. "Repent. For the Kingdom of Heaven is at hand." (Matt. 4:17)

Repentance is the legal process by which we step from the government of darkness into the government of God. Repentance is about stepping away from the lies and compromises that keep us from fully trusting in God. Repentance is how we align ourselves with the power and authority structure of Heaven.

This is not the gospel of 'get it right.' This is not where we pull out our whips, checklists and accountability partners. Behavior management focuses our attention on sin, but repentance restores intimacy with the Father. Purity is the fruit of intimacy. Spiritual authority is the result of that purity.

Intimacy —> Purity —> Authority

That's how repentance brings Kingdom.

This is precisely why the devil fears a pure and spotless Bride. Jesus demonstrated the power of a pure heart over the damage caused by rebellion and sin.

He cast out demons.

He raised the dead.

He healed everyone who came to him.

Early believers understood that purity in their hearts and purity in their fellowship empowered them to accomplish Christ's work of reconciliation on the Earth.

Consequently, the fellowship of believers wasn't open to just anyone. In fact, after Ananias and Sapphira died, "none of the rest [of the people, the **non-believers**] dared to associate with them; however, the people were holding them in high esteem and were speaking highly of them." (Acts 5:13, boldface mine) The early church carefully guarded the purity of their fellowship, so their authority would not be compromised.

As a result, the early church walked in the same power as Christ. People were healed. The dead were raised and the demonized set free.

It's been a few minutes since I raised anyone from the dead. But according to historians, this was the *normal Christian experience* for three hundred years![1]

Normal. For three hundred years. Stop and think about that.

Intimacy with Christ is how we war against the kingdom of darkness.

Significance or influence in the world system does not equate to spiritual authority. Many leaders have made it to the top saying all the right things, but the purity of their affection for Christ was over-shadowed by the love of money, power, or pleasure. Many are seduced and empowered by the idolatries of this age. As a result, they fall prey to immorality, greed and power. Or they sacrifice family for position, career, and money. They may have the capacity to achieve promotion, but they don't have the spiritual maturity to advance the Kingdom. Extending the blessing and influence of God's Kingdom doesn't happen when Christians occupy all the "right" seats of influence.

Our capacity to carry the culture of the Kingdom of God into the world flows from our intimacy with Christ. Intimacy with Christ is directly related to the quality of our trust (purity). Why? I won't be intimate with someone I don't trust.

Want more? Visit primalchurch.org for the free download on **Building Intimacy**.

---

1. Hyatt, E.L. (2002). 2000 Years of Charismatic Christianity : [a 21st century look at church history from a Pentecostal/Charismatic perspective]. Charisma House

Shifting Realities

As students, we gathered around to watch my science teacher scatter iron filings on a piece of paper. The disorganized mess of iron bits had no symmetry or beauty.

Then he positioned a magnet under the paper. In a millisecond, the iron filings snapped to attention along magnetic lines of force revealing a beautiful (and previously invisible) pattern.

Not only that, but the presence of the mother magnet actually changed the inner reality of every iron filing that came into proximal contact. It caused their *inner* structure to re-organize. The iron filings themselves *became* magnetic. Even after the magnet was removed, the filings continued to carry (in a small way) the power and authority structure inherited from the master magnet. They had been realigned. Proximity to the large magnet shifted their physical (internal) reality.

Those simple iron filings now carried the capacity to influence their surroundings.

That's what happens when the fellowship of believers gather with each other *and* Christ. In His Presence we become carriers of the power and authority structure of Heaven. Then we begin to manifest His influence, and that influence extends to everything around us. Even the earth.

The transformation of a lump of iron into a magnet illustrates how repentance and inner healing (alignment) activates believers. In order to restore the Primal Church, we must *first* align our internal reality with Christ. What holds the Bride back is not a structure or a program or a person. What restrains the Bride is a demonic force.

"For our struggle is not against flesh and blood [contending only with physical opponents], but against the rulers, against the powers, against the world forces of this [present] darkness, against the spiritual forces of wickedness in the heavenly (supernatural) places." Ephesians 6:12

We could also add, then, that our battle is not against buildings, programs, clergy, history or even Constantine. Every problem in the church is a *spiritual* problem with a *physical* manifestation. Moving from one denomination to another or from a large building to a small one does not itself solve anything. We'll just rebrand the same old thing in a different box. Knowledge alone won't fix the problem. A spiritual problem requires a spiritual response.

We can't be free of broken paradigms without undoing the compromises that landed us in the soup.

Only by repentance are we delivered from the demonic strongholds that keep us back.

What happened?

We've allowed the enemy's lies to slander the character of God and corrupt our trust in Him.

Where we've trusted anything else, we've allowed idolatry to compromise our intimacy (and our spiritual authority).

What must we do?

Ask the Holy Spirit to reveal where you have given the enemy permission, agreed with his lies or given space to idolatry. Repent as He brings those things to mind.

Ask the Holy Spirit to reveal the truth about God's heart.

Forgive those you need to forgive.

And, by the way, taking this journey in the company of other believers is a normal part of what it means to minister and be ministered to by the Body of Christ.

Section V
Set the Table

Now What?

While religious traditions and institutions might stand in the way, the primary challenge of this book is to you—the individual.

Before you move forward, take inventory. You can't step into a new chapter if you're hanging onto church-hurt. Ask the Holy Spirit to reveal who you need to forgive. Release anyone responsible for causing pain, for holding you back, or for disregarding Christ in you. Ask the Holy Spirit to purge your heart of bitterness, anger, rebellion, or retaliation. That poison will follow and interfere with connection and community. Be aware of these toxins—and avoid gathering with others who want to throw stones and rehearse grievances.

They aren't your tribe.

At the end of the day, learning to practice primal fellowship begins simply by practicing hospitality.

No service, no program, no agenda, no platform, no speaker. Primal Church is not an organization of members, it is an organic family of believers seeking to know Christ through each other.

God is a Father. He created families to be a picture of who He is. What happens in families becomes what happens in a nation. Our world and church are full of desperately lonely and broken people. Healthy families bring healing to those who never experienced a good father. Family-like relationships and the natural inter-dependence that results is the highest, best and simplest form of organization needed.

Look for people who are hungry for community and more of God's presence. Invite them over. Feed them. Pray for them. Listen to them. Lead the way into authentic and vulnerable communion.

Here are a few ways to start:

1. Take a sabbatical from programmatic, industrialized "Christian meetings" for 6 months or five years, or forever.

2. Practice hospitality.

3. When you're with other believers, ask: "What has God been teaching you?" or "How is your heart doing?"

4. Don't be afraid of silence.

5. Pray for each other spontaneously.

6. Do everyday stuff together: celebrate birthdays, share house projects, picnics and fire pits.

7. Be attentive to what the Holy Spirit is doing and saying.

8. Share testimonies.

9. Share hurt. Minister truth and inner healing.

10. Eat together.

11. Laugh together.

12. Play, work and serve together.

13. Expect Christ and the miraculous.

14. Fast spiritual fast food. These are spiritual meals made by others. Instead, do your own meal preparation. Don't lean on another person's relationship with God. Teaching and devotional materials aren't bad, but they can make you feel artificially full. Interact with Christ in the kitchen of your own life.

15. Ask the hard questions—heart questions. If our quest to understand God or His Word becomes purely cerebral, then we've lapsed into useless, air-headed, esoteric, theological-sounding mumbo jumbo. Sometimes a Bible study is used as a crutch to keep people from having to be vulnerable. If we're going to connect with God and each other, it has to involve our hearts. Doctrinal discussions and debates may sound impressive, but they keep hearts from engaging. (1 Cor. 8:1)

16. Fellowship is about meeting **with Christ** not meeting **about Christ**. The Gift of Christ in each other (spiritual gifts) are given so we might know Him and learn to depend on each other.

If I set myself to day-dreaming, I can picture a new (very old) expression of church as believers interact with each other and the Holy Spirit. Here in twos and threes. There by the half-dozen. Occasionally more than that. This doesn't have to be on a Sunday or the same day every week. **It doesn't have to be at the same place or even with the same people every time.** No denominational boundaries. No connection to a building or program. No carefully managed meetings. Just free, intentional and organic interaction with Christ in one another.

Seeking the fellowship of believers apart from an established program can feel illegitimate. History and tradition have programmed us to need the permission, blessing or covering from a "spiritual authority." But that idea is not in line with Scripture. Christ is your permission, your blessing, and your covering. Christ is the One who 'legitimizes' a gathering of believers. He has given us radical permission to connect—to really connect—anywhere, any time. Scripture says, where two or three gathered, He is there. (Matt. 18:20) The Bible does not say, where two or three are gathered under the spiritual covering of a local church authority.

Christ is the authority. His Presence is the point.

Be ready for those who worry about your salvation because you've stopped attending a program. They'll probably use Scripture to exhort you to not forsake the assembly of the saints. They might not get it. Be okay with that. What they think about you doesn't matter.

Remember, we can't solve the problem of organization with organization. The Primal Church can and must learn to function distinct from the institutions and organizations of men. The tendency to organize, codify, ritualize or otherwise 'manage' the experience of fellowship is often rooted in a desire to keep it predictable or to seek legitimacy. If you're looking to start a primal fellowship, don't tell people you are 'starting a church.' To do so immediately puts you under the burden of history and tradition. Do that and people will expect you—or someone else—to run the show.

Instead, all you need are hungry people willing to participate as fellow priests. If we struggle to grasp primal church, that is simply the result of looking at it through a religious grid. That grid needs constructs, formulas, structure and predictability. But primal church starts where we are authentic enough to find Christ in—and with—each other.

And that's enough.

Sacred Cows

Recognizing sacred cows can be difficult. These idols distract from what is most important and are not essential to our faith. Sacred cows often include an addiction to the opinions of man. Sacred cows can also include liturgies, ceremonies, buildings, organizations, community expectations, salaried roles, furniture, doctrinal positions, tithes, traditions and programs.

Cows evoke a pseudo-spiritual sentimentality that keeps us bound to traditions never Christ never sanctified.

So what do we do with all the buildings?

I knew someone would ask, but it is the wrong question. To get the right answer, we have to ask the right question.

The church has never been a building.

Christ's death made the sacrificial system and the temple obsolete. Christ offered the final sacrifice, and we are now the temple where the Holy Spirit lives.

Buildings are hungry. They demand to be fed. The money lender, the tax collector (in some cases), the utility providers, and maintenance teams all require money.

But the building is just a tool. And the overwhelming testimony from the last 1700 years is that it's the wrong tool for the job. At no point should our resources frame our mission. The innate requirements of 'church' buildings, programs and positions run counter to the needs of a family.

Resources (human and material) must serve the mission of Christ, not the other way around. If our organizational effort does *not* result in growing families of devoted disciples, then we must re-evaluate.

The simple fact that buildings and families need different things should give us pause. Buildings, programs and positions need butts in seats, financiers, staff and volunteers.

But disciples are made in families, not classrooms. Every time we try to institutionalize family we break it. It is impossible to institutionalize love. And love is the very essence of family.

Healthy spiritual mothers and fathers *reproduce* themselves—and the culture they carry—generationally.

Hungry and devoted followers of Christ need healthy spiritual families where they can interact personally with mothers and fathers. This looks like doing life together, not attending services together. A real church does anything and everything a family would do together: eat, garden, parent, worship, cook, eat, celebrate, serve, build stuff, share testimony and eat some more. It includes small groups in prayer and small groups making applesauce. In our experience, it is often intergenerational and flows easily from work to prayer to play.

Experiencing Christ in each other is, according to Scripture, the **primary** way we are to encounter and manifest the fullness of Christ. It is essential for spiritual formation and vital if the Church is going to complete her mission. We are the dwelling place (temple) of the Spirit of God. We are His favorite place to be! And as we join together, honoring (and putting a draw) on the Spirit of God in fellow believers, we get to experience everything the early church had at Her disposal. The spiritual family is (by God's design) organic, flexible and accessible to everyone.

If your first question is '*what do we do with the building?*' you'll miss the mark.

Don't ask a horse to push the cart.

Yes. Families grow slowly.

But slow winners are better than fast losers.

The great risk of a building is the cultural expectation already baked in for what happens inside. Because of long-held paradigms and the momentum of history, existing infrastructure *interferes* with the way God intends the Body to function. As such, the inertia of tradition makes the building a *very* dangerous thing indeed.

No one gets discipled in a pew. Seminaries do not make disciples. Discipleship isn't about increasing my knowledge; it's about increasing my *capacity* to walk with Christ and carry His influence into the world. Discipleship is about knowing God, not knowing about God. It's not about doctrinal correctness but about correctly expressing the essence of Christ.

Since Constantine, professional clergy and formal meeting places have devoured staggering quantities of wealth, time and energy. Sure, we could argue that a lot of good has been done through this institution.

It has!

If you're reading this, there's a chance you've been a part of some of that.

But let's unpack that line of thinking:

Children are a blessing from the LORD. That's scriptural. Everybody agrees. Fornication is sin. That is unbiblical. (Almost) everyone agrees.

If children (a blessing) result from sex outside of marriage (sin), does that suddenly validate the process?

Of course not.

In the same way, we can not validate or authenticate a process simply because some good has resulted. We must always go back to Scripture.

I'm not suggesting the modern system is immoral, simply that it is largely out of line with what Scripture teaches.

Does our way of 'doing church' allow for the multi-faceted expression of Christ in every believer?

If not, then it is at best inadequate or at worst an illegitimate expression of the church.

Let's not settle for the good and miss the best!

What about Professional Christians?

You'd be hard pressed to build a solid case from the New Testament for paid, professional church workers. Sure, salaried, 'professional' Christians *have* been the norm for the last seventeen hundred years, but if you were chasing *normal* Christianity, you wouldn't be reading this book.

While the apostle Paul certainly did not oppose compensating someone for their work, he went out of his way to make a point of his financial independence from the Church. (2 Cor. 2:17) The man who penned about twenty-five percent of the New Testament ran a small business to support himself. "For you remember, believers, our labor and hardship. We worked night and day [practicing our trade] in order not to be a [financial] burden to any of you while we proclaimed the gospel of God to you." (1 Thess. 2:9) While Paul occasionally received gifts and support, *occasional support* and hospitality does not establish a precedent for the full-time, paid minister model common in today's church construct.

Because all believers are priests, there is no need to create a salaried position. Consider what might happen if everyone gave a weekly gift of their time (instead of money) to serve each other. What would shift if we took all the money spent in the current system and put it towards meeting human need and solving problems? The world would sit up and take notice. (See John 13:35)

What about tithe?

Salaried religious leaders were never part of the Old Testament Temple system or the early church.

Even Old Testament priests, upon which our current model is supposedly based, did not work full-time at the temple. They were divided into groups and scheduled for three to five weeks of work per year. During that time they received a portion of the offerings to compensate for their service when they were on duty. Except for the high priest, they all depended on other occupations for their livelihoods.

The temple and sacrificial system was abolished by Christ, our High Priest. Now every believer is a temple, and every believer is a priest. (1 Pet. 2:9)

Tithe was collected to maintain the system that Christ abolished.

The New Testament encourages us to give generously but never tells us to tithe. Profound generosity is absolutely in character for a follower of Christ.

Currently, most of the money given by Christians is consumed by buildings, programs and salaries that have little to do with growing families of disciples. Without programs, our need for paid leadership dramatically shifts. If we do away with the building-centric model for Christian fellowship, we would free up resources to heal and bless our world.

Defining Church

Exactly what is church?

According to Scripture, there are two words that answer this question. The first term, *ekklesia*, is often translated "church". In general it refers to the Body of Christ, all believers or believers in a specific area. (Col. 1:18, Acts 9:31, 1 Cor. 1:2)[1] While we're not going to replicate an academic or comprehensive deep dive on a topic others have explored, the word originally could refer to any group or gathering of people—Christians or otherwise. (See Act 19:32 for ekklesia as referring to the mob provoked by a disgruntled silversmith.)

But never once does ekklesia refer to a building. Consequently, we have to change our language to line up with Scripture. We must stop using the word church to refer to a building, service, program, or institution.

---

1. Strongs's #1577: ekklesia – Greek/Hebrew Definitions – Bible Tools. (2025). Bibletools.org.https://www.bibletools.org/index.cfm/fuseaction/Lexicon.show/ID/G1577/ekklesia.htm

More important for the purposes of our discussion is the second word used for Church in the New Testament. This is the Greek word *koinonia*. This refers to *how* the Church functioned or what the *ekklesia did* when they got together. *Koinonia* carries the idea of participation in, or having a share of something. It involves mutual interaction, fellowship or intimacy.[2] It defined the spiritual, relational, and practical interconnection (communion) among those who belonged to Christ.

In the New Testament, the health of the Body (ekklesia) was *defined* by the material and spiritual substance of their connection (koinonia). That is the starting point for understanding primal church.

Many have forsaken the command to gather and encourage one another in favor of a Sunday meeting that requires nothing of them. (Hebrews 10:25)

At its core, then, the Church is more a verb than a noun.

Scripture says, they will know we are Christians by our love. (John 13:34-35) The nature of Christ is revealed, not by a connection to, or participation in a structured program, institution or activity. Instead, Christ is seen in the *nature* of our interaction with Him in each other. It is about experiencing Christ in each one another and expressing Him when we are together.

Generally speaking, the modern church attempts to be the ekklesia without koinonia. According to Scripture, this renders us impo-

---

2. Strongs's #2842: koinonia – Greek/Hebrew Definitions – Bible Tools. (2025). Bibletools.org . https://www.bibletools.org/index.cfm/fuseaction/Lexicon.show/ID/G2842/koinonia.htmvisited31/08/2021

tent and strips our capacity to carry the King's authority. Bottom line: meeting together and encountering Christ in each other are not the same thing. If your experience of Church is the usual three songs, a sermon, and the haphazard interaction you get before or after the main event, then you have a lot to look forward to!

Scripture says Christ is fully represented when *all parts of the Body* are engaged. (1 Cor. 12:12-27, Rom. 12-4-8)

We can not experience the full expression of Christ apart from communion with each other. (1 Cor. 12:27)

We can not grow and mature apart from the inter-action with Christ in each other. (Eph. 4:13)

We can not carry the redemption power of Christ into all creation without the maturity that comes from the gift of Christ exercised *for the common good*. (1 Cor. 12:7; Rom. 8:19)

We can not effectively witness to the lost without the tangible expression of familial love that results from the communion of saints with each other. (John 13:35)

And we can not testify to the rulers and authorities in heavenly places without first experiencing the multi-faceted wisdom of God in other members of the Body. (Eph. 3:10)

Since the Bible says only two people and Jesus need to be present to fully qualify—the fellowship of Christ is intensely personal and delightfully uncomplicated.

Anytime we meet with other believers, we have the opportunity to interact with the Spirit which they carry. This means we meet under His authority, His leadership, His influence, His agenda, at His pleasure and for His delight.

It becomes a treasure hunt where we look for and depend on the expression of Christ in each other.

Recommended Reading

Banks, R. J., & Banks, J. (1998). *The Church Comes Home: Building Community and Mission Through Home Churches.* Peabody, MA: Hendrickson Publishers.

Bartleman, F. (1980). *Azusa Street.* Plainfield, NJ: Logos International.

Eberle, H. R., & Trench, M. (2006). *Victorious Eschatology: A Partial Preterist View.* Yakima, WA: Worldcast Publishing.

Heidler, R. D. (2006). *The Messianic Church Arising!: Restoring the Church to Our Covenant Roots!* Denton, TX: Glory of Zion International Ministires.

Hogan, B. P. (2008) *There's a Sheep in My Bathtub: Birth of a Mongolian Church-Planting Movement.* Asteroidea Books.

HYATT, E. L. (2002). *2000 Years of Charismatic Christianity: A 21st-Century Look at Church History from a Pentecostal/Charismatic Perspective.* Lake Mary, FL: Charisma House.

Jacobsen, W. (2014). *Finding Church: What If There Really Is Something More?* Colorado Springs, CO: TrailView Media.

Kopp, D. (2023). The Emotional Dashboard: How to find peace in a world of crazy. D. Kopp. https://www.amazon.com/dp/0989585387

Pierce, C. D., & Heidler, R. (2015). *The Apostolic Church Arising: God's people gathering and contending for the glory today.* Denton, TX: Glory of Zion International Ministries.

Rossing, B. R. (2004). *The Rapture Exposed: The Message of Hope in the Book of Revelation.* New York, NY: Basic Books.

Rutz, J. H. (2005). *Megashift: Igniting Spiritual Power* (1st ed.). Colorado Springs, CO: Empowerment Press.

Shaw, S. B. (1905). *The Great Revival in Wales.* Chicago, IL: S. B. Shaw Publisher.

Viola, F. (2009). *Finding Organic Church: A Comprehensive Guide to Starting and Sustaining Authentic Christian Communities.* Colorado Springs, CO: David C. Cook.

Viola, F. (2004) The Untold Story of the New Testament Church: An extraordinary guide to understanding the New Testament. Shippensburg, PA: Destiny Image Publishers.

Viola, F., & Barna, G. (2012). *Pagan Christianity?: Exploring the roots of our modern church practices* (Rev. & Updated Ed.). Tyndale Momentum.

Acknowledgements

An under-baked book is not nearly as fun as a brownie in the same condition. So, we deeply appreciate the input of the early readers who braved the not-done version—and then told us why it wasn't done. Their insights and comments were invaluable. We would especially like to thank:

- Adam Grim
- Ben and Katie Fuller
- Emily Kopp
- Joanna Drexel-Blevins
- Linda Viselli
- Bob and Denise Botsford
- Isaiah Kopp

All opinions represent the authors, and any remaining errors are—of course—our own fault.

We are especially grateful for the feedback and interaction of the groups who joined us for the raw version of this study—whether in our living room or with the Botsfords! Your enthusiasm and connection to this new, but very-old way, continues to energize us.

About the Author

Dwight was born in Zambia but found his wife in America. Today, Dwight and Doe live in Lancaster County, where they've raised five children, run their businesses, tended a few chickens, written several books, and planted a garden.

They are always on the lookout for the real, the raw, and the enlightened—believers with dirt under their fingernails and a holy light in their eyes.

Adventure with us at primalchurch.org

www.ingramcontent.com/pod-product-compliance
Lightning Source LLC
Chambersburg PA
CBHW071231090426
42736CB00014B/3038